Climbing Psychology

Mind training for optimal climbing performance

Kevin Roet

With foreword by Dr Julia Frearson

First published 2021 by Kevin Roet
This edition is the second edition published 2023 by Kevin Roet

Published by Kevin Roet

978-1-5272-8768-6

Cover design: Mark Clubb www.carmarmedia.co.uk
Foreword: Dr Julia Frearson
Book design: Vicky Barlow www.victoriabarlow.co.uk
Editing: Sam Jersche www.sjediting.com
Illustrations: Marc Ward

Printed by Severnprint Ltd

Lary Arce on El Regreso con Gloria 8a, Hatûn Machay, Perú
Diego López

Foreword

As a trained clinical psychologist and teacher of yoga principles to climbers for the last decade, you could rightfully expect that I have mastered my mind when it comes to the psychology of climbing. But this is the thing – I notice my mind, I nurture it, and I accept it, but I still struggle to face my fearful thoughts and excel at my favourite sport.

I have known Kev, the author of this ace book, for many years now. At first, just a face at the local climbing gym and then as someone who showed me support and shared his wisdom to help me face my fears. I sought his advice on many occasions and benefited from informal encouragement before undertaking a short course with him aimed at helping me overcome a fear of falling. The course was successful, and I had overcome my fear; however, over time, I stopped practising what I had learnt and retreated into my 'threat brain' again. This book serves as an indispensable reminder of all he has taught me over the years, bringing it all back at the turn of a page.

Kev is an inspiration to others in his climbing community. Its been an honour to have an early view of this excellent book, which brings together complex ideas and techniques into a readable and practical guide to developing as a climber.

This book captures the essence of the body-mind approach that I have tried to espouse in my combination of yogic and scientific theory and practice over the years. One of my personal and professional passions is understanding the impact of neurobiology on our habits, including how we think. Simply put, the repeated rehearsal of anxious or perfectionistic behaviour and associated thinking styles leads to a quick descent into worrisome and unhelpful patterns in stressful circumstances. It's a self-fulfilling prophecy, but not in an abstract way – in a genuine and scientifically understood way. The only way out of this cycle is to practice and practice (and practice some more) alternative ways of living and being. As the yogis say, change is "99% practice and 1% theory". Many people talk about wanting something to be different but do very little to change it.

This book is underscored with genuine compassion for the anxiously wired brain; it provides evidence-based and considered wisdom that we can overcome fear. It provides enough science to motivate you to start making changes and then takes your hand while you ride the journey to the freedom offered by mindfulness of the moment. The techniques are presented in bite-sized chunks that can be applied to your climbing, allowing you to progress steadily and gain confidence. Most of all, the book asks you to notice yourself. Notice and practice being different. As a psychologist, yoga teacher and climber – I urge you to heed this advice, and in the words of a famous yoga guru, "all is coming".

Dr Julia Frearson

Introduction

There I was, palms sweating as if waiting for my moment on stage. I felt like I was having an out-of-body experience; my anxiety was building up in my stomach. My skin tingling with fear. My breath was getting shorter with every moment that went by, fully anticipating what would happen next. The drive to want to face my fears became stronger. I held on so tight, like a parent holding his/her child's hand crossing a busy road. It was now or never.

I decided to open my eyes halfway up a loop-the-loop on a rollercoaster ride at the age of 12, only to realise my fear did not seem so scary. "What else is not so scary." I thought to myself. I had been scared of many things as a child, but this is the first profound memory I have, where I feel I had overcome fear all by myself.

That experience helped me build self-confidence and realise that what may feel scary at first is not all that it seems.

Climbing is such an amazing sport; the sense of adventure and potential for overcoming adversity.

As climbers, we train physically using fingerboards, core exercises, antagonist training, pull-ups, campusing, power endurance, etc. We train our technique. But why, when a large part of climbing is psychological, do we tend to forget about this part?

I had an experience in my earlier years of climbing where I had lost all of my confidence; fear of falling became a hindrance and held me back. It affected my drive, my emotions, and I stopped enjoying climbing at times. I had to change something within me and build up my confidence again.

Through years of reading, research and self-analysis, I came up with ways of dealing with fear/anxiety; my climbing improved. I realised we do not need to be stuck in a rut where we feel we may never make progress.

All you need is a willingness to learn, have the ability to listen to yourself, and be patient. You can have a physically not so strong climber with a strong mental game, and they will surpass all we think is possible.

In this book, you will learn how the brain works. You will discover that the brain is malleable, and we can train it to do anything we put our minds to. We will look at the fear of falling, the fear of failure, and the influence of thought.

The concept of the book is that with some self-awareness, we can train ourselves step-by-step to deal with these aspects of climbing. We live in a society where we focus on the end result but aren't always sure how to get there. Through breathing, gradual exposure, regular practice and a willingness to learn, we can achieve so much more than we think we are capable of.

After dealing with my fears, I realised I was not the only one who suffered anxieties with their head game. So I compiled a course to try and help others. I have been running 'The Climbing Psychology Workshop' through my company, Rise & Summit, for 5–6 years now and had amazing results. The book is a compilation of research and personal experience to share with you and help you on your way to dealing with your anxieties in climbing. I have tried to simplify each subject as you could easily fill a book on each.
I have kept it relevant and concise.

Have fun reading it.

Note: I am not a psychologist, nor do I profess to be. I am an obsessive climber and climbing instructor with a great awareness of myself and others in a climbing situation. A doctor in psychology has verified the content of the book.

Contents

Balcarce, Argentina
Jeff Ochoa

Statement of risk

Read the following before you use this book.

Climbing is an activity which carries an element of risk, which can result in personal injury or death. Participants in these activities should be aware of and accept these risks and be responsible for their own actions and involvement. The information in this book is not intended to encourage you to take unacceptable risk, but to provide you with information on how you can deal with stress/fear better in a climbing situation. The aim should be learning about yourself and create a better understanding of how your brain works scientifically and psychologically.

Climbing safely requires good judgement and proper technique, gained through experience, sound advice and instruction. If you are unsure on any aspect of this book, seek instruction from a qualified professional. The advice given in this book are the author's opinions. The author and publisher of this book do not accept responsibility or liability for any accident, injury, loss or damage sustained while following any of the techniques described in this book.

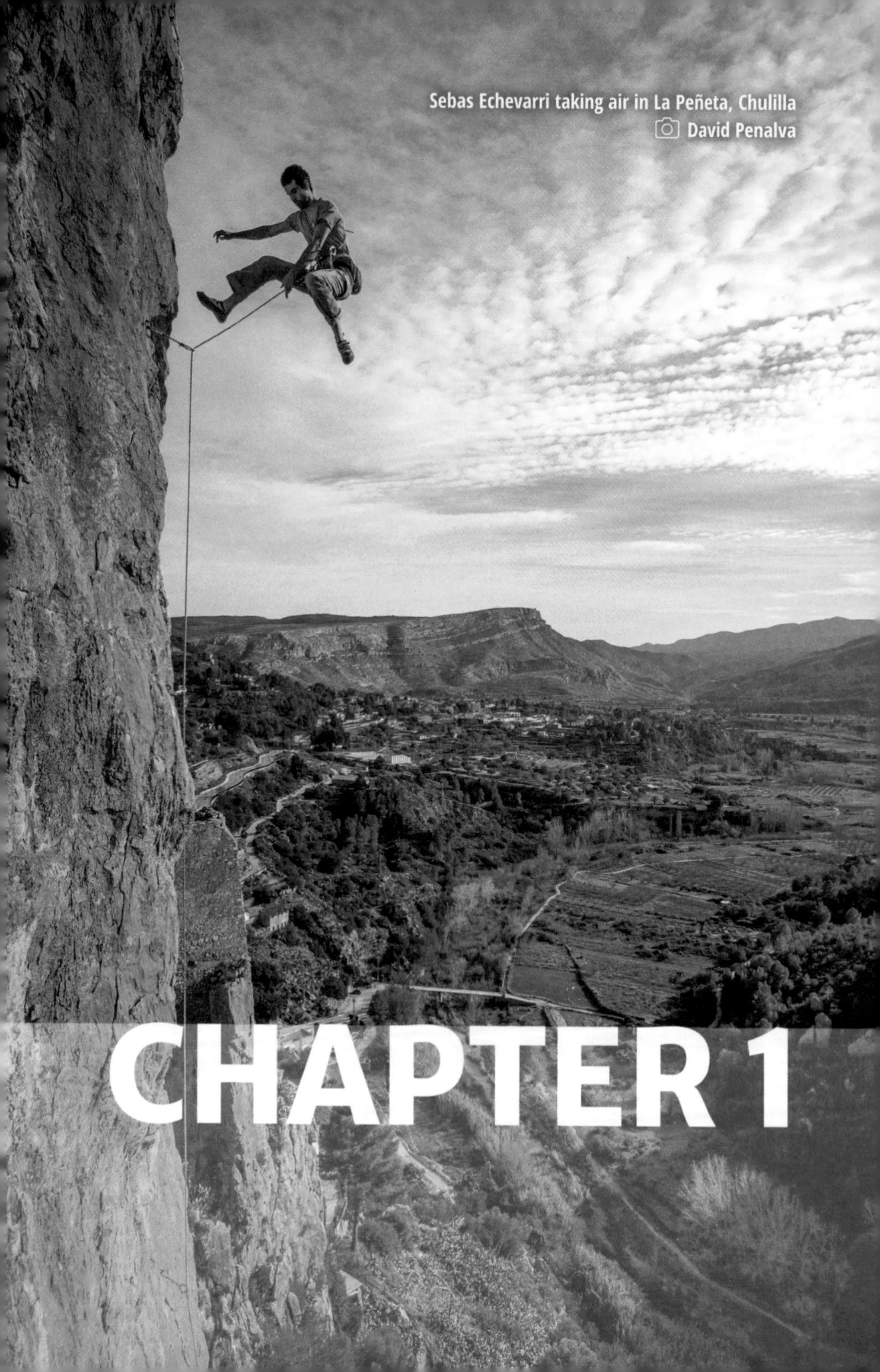

Sebas Echevarri taking air in La Peñeta, Chulilla
David Penalva

CHAPTER 1

Fear and the Brain

"Avoiding danger is no safer in the long run than outright exposure. The fearful are caught as often as the bold."

HELEN KELLER

A man goes to his psychiatrist to face his fears. Ever since he was a child, he feared that someone was under his bed at night.

"Every time I go to bed, I think there is someone under it. I'm scared. I think I'm going crazy." Explains the man.

"I can help you there." says the psychiatrist. "Come and see me three times a week for a year, and we should be able to get rid of those fears."

"How much do you charge?" asks the man.

"Fifty pounds per visit." asserts the psychiatrist.

"I'll sleep on it, and if needed, I'll come back to you."

Six months later, the psychiatrist met the man on the street. "Why did you not come and see me about those fears you were having?" asked the psychiatrist.

"Well, £50 per visit, three times a week for a year is a lot of money.

A barman cured me for £10. I was so happy to have saved all this money I bought myself a classic car."

"Is that so" expressed the psychiatrist, slightly annoyed. "And how, may I ask, did the barman cure you?"

"He told me to cut the legs off the bed – there's certainly no one under there now."

Fear can be a funny thing. We may not always be able to cure the fear itself, but we can certainly develop ways to deal with it. This chapter talks about fear and may at times be very scientific. It is here to give you some background about what happens in the brain and provide you with some understanding. Please do not feel that you need to remember it all word for word as there is a lot of information to process.

WHAT IS FEAR?

Fear is a feeling induced by a threat or danger; This can either be a real threat (an injury or life-threatening situation) or a perceived threat (a new or unfamiliar situation, a learnt habit, or a blueprint set in our minds). By "perceived threat", I specifically mean when we think something is threatening or dangerous when in reality you may actually be safe. This book will concentrate on perceived danger, the non-life-threatening, irrational fear that occurs when climbing.

By describing this type of fear as irrational, I am in no way trying to discredit the feeling you get when you are scared in certain climbing situations. I am objectively trying to describe the fear we feel when in no real danger of injury or death (i.e., climbing above a clip 10 metres up or making an insecure move three-quarters of the way up a route where we are unsure of the outcome).

Fear was responsible for our early ancestors' survival. It helped us, as human beings, survive the onslaught of predatory animals. If we did not run, hide, or outsmart bigger or dangerous animals/situations, we would likely have met our destiny in our early existence. So, fear is a good thing even though it can get in the way of our daily lives.

WHAT HAPPENS IN THE BRAIN?

Fear is the result of a chemical chain reaction that occurs in the brain within a few milliseconds. It starts with a conscious or sub-conscious stressful stimulus and ends with the release of chemicals resulting in fast breathing, a racing heart, and the constriction of blood vessels close to the skin. Vital organs are flooded with nutrients and oxygen, and the larger muscle groups are energised as they get pumped with blood. This state is also known as the fight-or-flight response.

A small part of our brain structure, called the Amygdala, is at the centre of decoding stressful stimuli. It also stores this information so the next time you find yourself in a similar situation, it will remember what path to follow.

Below (Diagram 1.1) is a picture of the brain, indicating the areas of the brain involved in the fear response process.

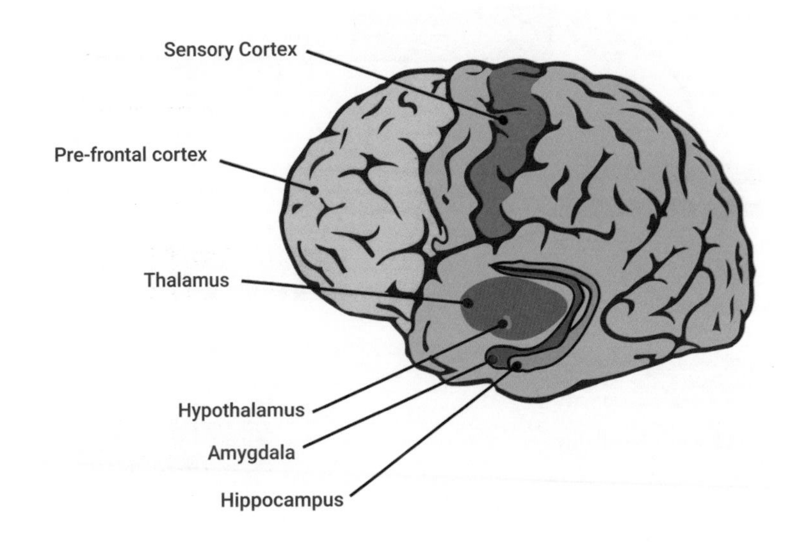

Diagram 1.1 The areas of the brain involved in the fear response process

Thalamus – relays motor and sensory information (from eyes, ears, mouth and skin) to the cerebral cortex (outer layer of the brain).
Somatosensory or Sensory cortex – interprets the aforementioned sensory data.
Hippocampus – associated mainly with memory, particularly long-term memory. The organ also plays a vital role in spatial navigation, learning, and emotions.
Amygdala – responsible for the perception of emotions such as anger, fear, sadness, and control of aggression. It also stores memories attached to fear.
Hypothalamus – links the nervous system to the endocrine system (the body's hormones); it also activates the "fight-or-flight" response.

Signals take several pathways in the brain. This book will focus primarily upon two pathways due to their influence on how we experience and manage fear.

The first is the short path, which can be described as the 'act-now-ask-questions-later' path; the second is the longer path, namely, the 'let's-analyse-this-fear-before-reacting' path. Both processes happen simultaneously.

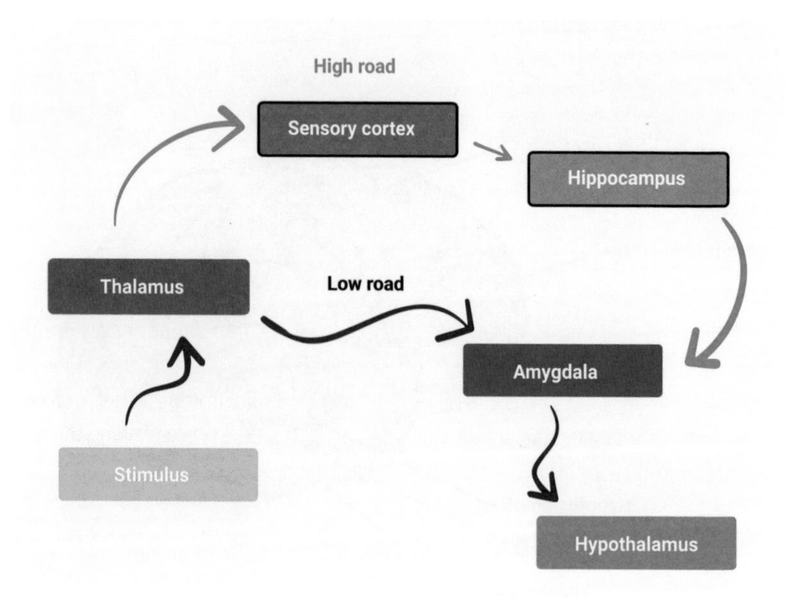

Diagram 1.2 The paths involved in the fear process

Fearful stimuli, whether real or perceived, trigger signals from the body's senses that are then sent to the thalamus. From here, the signal can travel two ways, as described above. The short path or low road (the act-now-ask-questions-later path) is the quickest response to a situation, where a signal is sent straight to the amygdala, which in turn sends a signal to the hypothalamus and initiates the fight-or-flight response.

Simultaneously, neural signals are travelling the long-way-around or the high road (the let's-analyse-this-fear-before-reacting path). Information gets passed to the somatosensory cortex from the thalamus. Here the sensory input is interpreted and sent through to the hippocampus, where the threat is given context and compared to previous situations/threats. The hippocampus is the brain's memory bank. If the hippocampus considers the threat real, a signal is sent to the amygdala and then to the hypothalamus, where it readies the body for a fight-or-flight response. Alternatively, if the hippocampus decides the threat is not real, it will quieten down the amygdala, and a signal is sent to the hypothalamus to say everything is fine.

> *An example of this response may be when at the local climbing centre while talking to a friend; you catch a glimpse of a shadow moving above your head. You immediately think someone is falling in your direction. All of your senses heighten, but as you turn around you realise it was only the lights casting a shadow from another part of the room. You relax, as you realise there is no threat; these processes happen simultaneously, which is why you sometimes experience a moment when you freeze before reacting.*

The amygdala stores memories linked with fear. In certain situations where the amygdala considers a perceived threat linked with a past experience, it will send a signal to the hypothalamus and allow the body to react without further analysis. For example: imagine you were bitten on the leg by a snake while walking through long grass in the past. You are walking through similar length grass today, and your leg brushes up against a stick, giving you a similar sensation as to when the snake bit you. Your amygdala would send a message to the hypothalamus, causing you to react straight away by jumping out of the way.

Melissa Clements at The Warehouse Climbing Centre – trying hard
📷 Hannah Williams

When a signal isn't life-threatening, as, with the majority of climbing situations, the brain takes the more rational 'let's-analyse-this-fear-before-reacting' path. Suppose you see something that is not life-threatening but still frightening – i.e., you are above a quickdraw/runner or on an overhang – in that case, the amygdala alerts the somatosensory (or sensory) cortex. The sensory cortex alerts the hippocampus and spurs it to compare the current threat to past ones (scripts explain these further in chapter 2). If it determines that the present fear stimulus is a threat but not life-threatening, the hippocampus heightens your senses and triggers your fight-or-flight response through the amygdala.

The fight-or-flight response from the hypothalamus activates two systems. The first is the sympathetic nervous system, which uses nerve pathways to speed up the body, tense up, and become more alert. It also sends signals to the adrenal gland to stimulate the release of epinephrine (adrenaline) and

Ben Clayton-Jolly on South West ridge of Stuedlgrat
Dave Talbot

norepinephrine (noradrenaline) into the bloodstream. The second is the adrenal-cortical system, which uses the adrenal cortex to release around 30 different hormones through the bloodstream to get the body ready to deal with threats.

The release of these hormones has the following effects on the body:

- Increased blood pressure
- Increased heart rate
- Increased glucose levels in the bloodstream
- Arteries and veins close to the skin constrict to allow more blood flow to the major muscle groups
- Potential to start sweating
- Systems, such as the digestion system, shut down to allow more energy supply to what is thought to be essential functions in the situation
- Pupils dilate
- Muscles tense up
- The brain focuses on what is essential in the situation (usually one thing)
- The muscles surrounding the respiratory system relax to allow for increased oxygen intake by the lungs.

Although these effects can be very beneficial in a real survival situation they are not so beneficial in climbing. Some of the responses associated with the 'fight or flight' response in climbing may be:

- Forgetting left and right
- Not being able to see the holds
- Disco legs
- Backing off
- Feeling upset or angry
- Can't move up or down (freeze response)
- Unable to think clearly
- Our mind may go blank

Did you know that the physiological feeling of fear and excitement are closely related? Whether excited or scared, the hypothalamus instructs the body to increase respiration rate and heart rate, dilate the pupils, and trigger sweaty palms. Both feelings trigger the same systems within the body; the only difference is how your brain translates the situation.

CORTISOL

Cortisol is a stress hormone produced in the adrenal gland. Fearful situations trigger the hypothalamus to produce high levels of cortisol that, in turn, causes the fight-or-flight response. Some people produce higher cortisol levels than others in a given situation. Studies have shown that early childhood trauma can affect the size of the amygdala, the hippocampus, the hypothalamus, amongst a few. It can also influence the connectivity between all of these parts, hence reduce the capacity to cope with subsequent stressful events. I mention this because some people are more sensitive to situations where higher cortisol and adrenaline levels are produced.

> *Steve and Karen decided to go ice climbing in Cogne, a small sleepy village in the Italian Alps and an ice climbing mecca.*
> *There are hundreds of ice falls with easy access from the valley floor. Karen, a weathered, experienced winter, alpine, and ice climber, wanted to show Steve the ropes and give him an experience of a lifetime. Steve, a strong sport climber, was always up for anything.*
> *Unbeknownst to Karen, Steve had had a troubled past. As they have only known each other for a few months, Steve had not opened up yet.*
> *The cracking noises echoed through the darkness of the Valnontey Valley as their boots hit the frozen and compacted snow on the path. As they approached their chosen route, the sun trying to creep over the ridgeline, like a child pulling themselves over a high fence, brought them a sense of comfort. Karen set off to climb the first pitch; she managed this with ease and set up an anchor.*
> *"On belay," she shouts, taking in the slack rope like an umbilical cord providing a sense of belonging and comfort.*
> *As the sun creeps around the mountain, a few of her rays start to heat some of the ice sections. Steve picks up his ice axes and psyches himself up.*
> *Just as he is about to set off, a chunk of ice falls beside him, triggering a level of adrenaline and cortisol that causes him to freeze. Steve tries to relax and breathe but is unable to lower the levels of anxiety; he communicates with Karen that he wants to go back.*

If we wish to change something we feel fearful about, we need to understand how our bodies and minds react to the situations we put ourselves in when climbing. If we want to overcome a fear, we need to deal with stress in manageable chunks (see Chapter 3 – Comfort zone and Risk zone), however small these changes may feel.

Karen and Steve spend the rest of the day in a café, talking and having a heart to heart.
Steve opened up about his past and felt Karen was able to hold his emotions. The story has a happy ending, as Karen and Steve build up the difficulty of routes over their stay and conclude their holiday with the first route they had abandoned, with Steve leading the last pitch.

Andrew Finney on 'Heading the Shot' (7a+), Seamstress Slab, Serengeti
Luca Celano

THE FREEZE RESPONSE

So far, we have only talked about the fight-or-flight response. Although, sometimes, when faced with a threat, our bodies may choose a third option – a state of attentive immobility, freeze – a built-in defence mechanism, where we appear to do nothing.

We all remember the scene from the film 'Snatch', where Turkish and Tommy escort Mickey O'Neil out of the backdoor after the final fight scene (Where Brick Top gets shot), and all Turkish and Tommy can do is 'freeze' (1 hour and 34 minutes in, definitely worth a watch if you haven't already).

Freezing does not seem helpful, right! At least with fight-or-flight, we may have a chance of escaping the 'danger'. So why does it happen? First, a brief science lesson to explain the Autonomic Nervous system.

Autonomic Nervous system

The Autonomic Nervous system (ANS) is a control system that regulates bodily functions like heart rate, respiratory rate, pupils, digestion, sweat, saliva production, to name a few. It is the main mechanism in control of basic physiological functions to help us adapt to our environment.

The ANS consists of two main parts, the Parasympathetic Nervous system (PSNS) and the Sympathetic Nervous system (SNS).

Usually working together in harmony, these have some opposing functions (see diagram opposite). The Sympathetic Nervous system responds to perceived threats by increasing arousal, whereas the Parasympathetic Nervous system controls the rest and digest functions.

When 'freezing', both the SNS and PSNS are activated simultaneously; however, the PSNS is dominant, counterbalancing the physical effects of the fight-or-flight response causing us to 'relax', or in this case, 'freeze'. Our heart rate and respiratory rate slow down; we may even hold our breath.

It is an automatic survival mechanism that we have no control over. It is the body trying to protect us physically and psychologically by 'playing dead'. It helps us disassociate from the situation and pumps the body full of pain-relieving hormones. Our brains shut down, our memory can be affected, our perception of reality can be altered, and our perception of stress is magnified. Possibly helpful in a real life-or-death situation, but certainly not in climbing.

This response is completely out of our control and happens automatically. It is not a conscious decision we make. It doesn't matter whether you are a highly skilled martial arts expert, or big and muscly. Anyone can experience the feeling of 'freezing'.

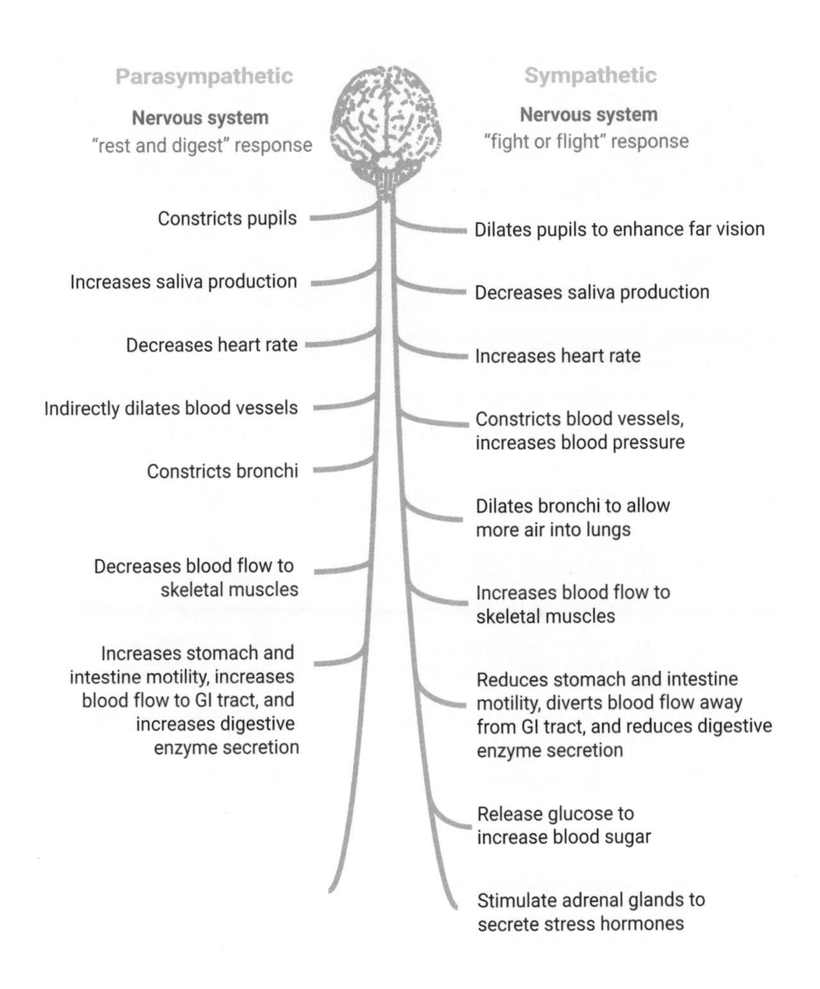

Diagram 1.3 Functions of the parasympathetic and sympathetic nervous systems

WHAT CAN WE DO WHEN WE ARE SCARED?

Having explained fear and how it manifests itself in our brain and bodies, what can we do about it? How do we deal with it?

In order to bring the body back to homeostasis (internal balance) after an adrenaline/cortisol fuelled situation, we can use the PSNS.

The PSNS will reverse fight-or-flight responses; this is referred to as the *rest and digest system*. We can artificially stimulate the PSNS through breathing (chapter 8), or visualisation. Although dependant to which extent we experience fear, if it is too much outside of our comfort zone initiating the PSNS may be harder to impossible.

Remember, fear is a good thing; it is responsible for keeping us alive, but it can also prevent our climbing progress. When climbing, if the individual perceives the experience of fear to be real, an extreme response may lead to losing control over the situation.

So, when we are trying to change and manage our perception of fear, we need to become aware of the paths our brain follows (see Chapter 2 – Scripts and Behavioural Patterns) and operate on the edge of our comfort zone (discussed further in chapter 3).

The following chapters will explain how we can use small steps to change our instinctual or learnt behaviours. There is no magic wand; you must continually work on yourself in order to progress. It may feel uncomfortable at times, but keep persisting, and the results will follow. Remember that all the climbers you may think have no fear, experience fear. They will have worked on coping mechanisms to deal with it in their own way.

EXERCISE 1.1

Write down the elements within climbing that cause you to feel fear. The more honest you are with yourself, the more helpful this will be.
List as many items as you can.

Here are a few examples to start you off:

- Climbing above the last clipped quickdraw
- Being positioned on an insecure move/hold
- Being high up
- Being belayed by a new belayer
- Clipping onto an insecure move/hold
- Climbing a slab
- Climbing an overhang

The more comprehensive this list is, the easier it will be to understand your internal workings and start making changes.

Black Stallion – 8B /V13 (FA)

Sharad Chandra Khiyali

"I CLIMB EVERYTHING WHICH INSPIRES ME TO CLIMB. I LOVE THE PROCESS OF FINDING NEW ROCKS TO CLIMB. IT'S LIKE A CONSTANT URGE TO SEARCH FOR THE HIDDEN TREASURE, SEEKING FOR THOSE LINES WHICH ARE HARD, POSSIBLE AND PURE."

SANDEEP KUMAR MAITY

Cade Prior

CHAPTER 2

Scripts and Behavioural Patterns

"A habit cannot be tossed out the window; it must be coaxed down the stairs a step at a time."

MARK TWAIN

"Focus on your feet," Emily said to herself, approaching an overhang. She's breathing heavily, fuelled on adrenaline, fear, and uncertainty. "Don't hold your breath; keep moving." She narrowly makes the next quickdraw and sighs with a sense of relief. She can feel her body relax a little. "I have to climb this overhang; I hate overhangs!" Her forearms feel pumped, "I can't feel them", "I'm going to fall!" Fear has become so intense; she is unable to move. "Take!".

Emily repeated this process many times, creating an expectation within herself every time she climbed an overhanging route. The same script, repeated over time, confirmed this neural pathway and laid down the foundations for a newly learnt habit.

There are approximately 86 billion neurons in our brain. From the day we are born, there is a continual process of learning. When neurons regularly fire together in a particular sequence due to repetition, emotional and behavioural habits begin to form. Our lives are full of them, both good and bad!

A habit is an automated process where the brain has laid down a pathway for an electrical impulse to follow, saving energy, so we do not consciously have to think about it. The brain is lazy that way! The brain is around 2% of the total body's weight but consumes on average around 20% of your total daily energy intake. So, if it can save energy somewhere along the way by automating a process, it will.

Take, for example, when we go to open a door handle. When at the age of 1 or 2, we first tried to open a door using the handle, it would have taken a lot of conscious processing to work this out. Now that we are a bit older, our eyes relay the information to our brains, comparing this with the previous door handles we have experienced. It will then translate that information to the part of our brain, that controls the muscles in our hand/arm, and open the door without consciously having to think about it.

The same pattern recognition process occurs in climbing, where we will have developed an array of good and bad habits. Let's take Sam, he has been climbing for 3 years, and occasionally struggles with an element of self-belief. Every time Sam climbs and ends up on an insecure move, he decides not to attempt the move and instead downclimbs until the rope goes tight. He has repeated this process so many times that his mind has constructed an automated procedure, which he performs every time he finds himself in a similar situation.

Alex Burns on Flying Buttress Direct (E1, 5b), Stanage Edge
Dave Talbot

While this information is interesting and may shed light on some of our automated and sometimes unconscious behaviours, there is light at the end of the tunnel. We can unlearn bad or unwanted habits, with conscious effort and awareness.

A habit is a sequence of behaviours (script) which play out given a certain situation, based on knowledge and information we have stored in our mind (schemas).

Let's look at schemas and scripts in more detail.

SCHEMA

Frederic Bartlett, a British psychologist, first came up with the concept of mental structures within the brain. Jean Piaget, a Swiss psychologist, later named these '*schemas*'. Schemas (or schemata) are blueprints/assumptions our mind makes to enable us to process information efficiently and make judgements in everyday life. A pre-existing mental concept that helps us to organise and interpret information. These are based on our experiences and may or may not be accurate. For example, we may assume that someone from a specific cultural background has a certain way of being/behaving. Assuming all Dutch people are rude (straight talkers), or all English people beat around the bush and don't get to the point. If we take Emily's example, the schema here is her dislike for overhangs.

> *The first time Emily climbed an overhang, she felt pushed by her friends, who thought she would enjoy the challenge. She was not so experienced at the time, and felt pushed into it, but did not want to disappoint her friends. She tried, but fear got the better of her. She felt disappointed with her performance, and told herself she disliked overhangs. Unaware, she was laying down the beginnings of a schema. By repeating this process, she reinforced this schema, her belief of disliking overhangs.*

Schemas can be beneficial but can also hinder us and prevent progress, as we may fall back into prior knowledge rather than trying to create a new understanding of a concept. Current cognitive framework (schemas) can also affect how we perceive or create further schemas, and create a bias in the way these are formed, focusing only on whatever attests our pre-existing beliefs and ideas.

SCRIPT

A script is an expected sequence of schemas for a given situation, played out over time – An automated behavioural pattern, which the mind follows, based on historical information and experiences stored in our minds. Scripts can describe patterns in our behaviour, thoughts and emotions.

Every time Ben climbs above a runner where he thinks he may fall or a certain emotion has been linked to this situation, his mind takes over and the rest of the script follows. In this case, the script may involve downclimbing, holding the runner or quickdraw, or shouting "take". Scripts refer to the part of our mind that has created an expected pattern set within all of us, to make our mind work more efficiently, so we have more energy spare to spend elsewhere.

HOW DO WE CHANGE SCRIPTS?

To change a script, we need to follow the following steps:

1. We need a willingness to make changes
2. Become self-aware of the pattern your mind follows
3. Choose an alternative script
4. Start by delaying the old script
5. Try to execute the new pattern in small digestible chunks on easier terrain
6. Repeat step 3–5 over and over again until the process becomes automated
7. Now practice it under stress (build this up slowly, see step 5. If you do this step too early, your mind will want to revert to its old script)

Before we tackle making any changes in our behavioural pattern within climbing, we need a willingness to make changes; this may feel uncomfortable at first. Even the thought of trying to change something we generally avoid may cause us anxiety or butterflies. Please don't worry; I'll be here on your journey with you.

To change a script, we need to become aware of the pattern(s) that our mind likes to follow; this involves realising that there is a pattern that happens of which we may not be aware. We must look at ourselves and analyse whether these are positive or negative patterns; this may feel awkward, especially if we are not used to it.

Next time you go climbing, try to consciously identify a pattern you may follow in a given situation. Ask your friend (belayer) to help you with this. Try using positive language when describing this (see Chapter 6 – The Influence of Thought). Sometimes you may not be aware of these, but after a climb (back on the ground or at the top of a pitch), take a moment to analyse the patterns your mind has just executed. Again, be patient with yourself; this process can be very uncomfortable, and may take some practice to get an understanding. Remember your motivation for doing so.

If we take the previous example, feeling scared when we climb above a quickdraw and downclimb, to create comfort (see Chapter 3 – comfort and risk zone), it feels like a big step to admit that there is a negative pattern we follow in this scenario.

EXERCISE 2.1

Write below three patterns you follow, in a climbing situation, which you would like to change.

Once we are aware of the pattern we follow in specific scenarios, we can choose a different path; one we would like to follow when you are not under stress, i.e., when on the ground.

Next time you are climbing, catch yourself when you are about to follow an old script, then try to replace this with the new script. Doing this may feel tricky initially. Even delaying your usual (old script) pattern is progress. Staying in the position from which you would usually downclimb to your comfort zone and staying there for a few seconds help create the initial change. Combine this with the coping strategies explained in chapter 10 and breathing techniques described in chapter 8. Remember, slowly build this up over time.

> A rich man once asked an old, wise man to help his son change his bad habits. The old man asked his son to take a walk with him through the garden. After taking a few steps, the wise man stopped and asked the young man to pull a small flower out of the ground.
> The young man grabbed the plant with his fingers and easily plucked it out. The wise man nodded, and they resumed walking.
> A few seconds later, they stopped again, and the wise man pointed towards another plant a bit larger than the last. The young man grabbed it with his hand and plucked it out of the ground with a bit of effort. "Now pluck out that one," the wise man said, pointing towards a bush. The young man grabbed the bush with both hands and, using all of his strength, barely managed to pluck it out of the ground.
> "Now you see that small tree, there? Try and pluck that one." The young man grabbed the trunk with both hands, pulled as hard as he could, but he couldn't even move it.
> "It's impossible, master. I can't do it."
> "You see, my boy, it's the same with our habits. If we let them grow and take root, it becomes harder and harder for us to stop them."

When trying to create and execute new patterns, make sure these are performed in small digestible chunks and situations where no stress is involved (see comfort and risk zone – Chapter 3). Repeat this process as many times as you need to; you will find yourself making progress.

Suppose we take the previous example of Sam downclimbing from an insecure move. We can assume Sam feels uncomfortable with the unknown and the possibility of falling. Sam wants to make changes, so he decides he is going

EXERCISE 2.2

Write down below what scripts you would like to change corresponding to the above behavioural pattern and divide them into steps.

For example, if we take the example of Emily, who struggles with overhangs, she can take the following digestible steps:

- Climb up to overhang, at the point where anxiety may be high, stay for 5–10 seconds, trying to breathe and relax, before sitting on the rope.
- Repeat the above step until it feels comfortable, build up to just let go without sitting on rope
- Try one more move, then let go. Repeat until it becomes easier.
- Try two moves, then let go. Repeat until it becomes easier.

Now it's your turn.

to tackle it. Next time he is on an insecure handhold, he decides to stay there for 5 seconds and tries to relax the best he can before downclimbing. A small change, right, but change nonetheless – the building blocks for a new pattern.

As well as working on insecure moves, he is also practicing progressive falling on every session. Two months go by, and he has built up his confidence a little and is now able, from an insecure handhold, to take a leap of faith, dynamically move up to touch the next hold, then fall off.

The time it may take to change behavioural patterns is very individual; this depends on your personality, past experiences, cultural aspects, etc. One person may need to practice something 20 times to lay down some change, whereas someone else may need to repeat the process 100 times to experience the same level of change.

Just make sure you are patient with yourself. This process can take a long time, and if you create too much stress, your mind will naturally want to revert to what it knows, i.e., the old pattern. The importance here is "BITE-SIZE CHUNKS". You wouldn't ask a 9-a-day coffee addict to go cold turkey from one day to the next; that's asking for trouble.

According to Phillippa Lally (2012), a health psychology researcher at University College London, it takes around 66 days for a new behaviour to become a habit. That would mean climbing daily with purposeful practice. Then there is Malcolm Gladwell's (2008) theory which states that to become an expert or master something takes 10,000 hours of practice, which he explains in his book "Outliers". I'm not asking you to practice falling in climbing for 10,000 hours. Just compare the amount of time you spend climbing to the amount of time you spend on your head game and practicing falling. A big disparity, right!

What we can derive from these two theories is that forming habits requires purposeful practice on a regular basis. Also, the process must be repeated until it becomes an unconscious automated process. Again, the frequency and quantity we need to practice are very individual as mentioned before.

Please do take the above statement with a pinch of salt. We are all different, and these timings will depend on your character, how long you have had the habit you are trying to change, the experiences you have had in your life, and any trauma linked with the situation, etc.

One great way of keeping track of our progress is by writing a diary or having a wall chart where each time you go climbing, you work a little bit on the script you would like to change. This way, you can see that progress is happening over a longer period and can see that the hard work you are putting in is worthwhile – a motivator to keep going.

TRAUMA

Why do I want to talk about trauma? Trauma can affect scripts in the mind in two ways. It can influence the way a new script is formed (i.e. historic trauma affecting current forming of a new script). It can also affect an already set script, negatively (i.e. witnessing a bad climbing accident). These would need more patience to create change.

This trauma can have an affect on climbing-related scripts and may or may not have originated from a climbing-related incident. It can be very individual as to how this information is logged or processed, meaning that the same situation may affect two individuals very differently and to a very different extent. These could be characteristics of the individuals, their developmental processes, the meaning of the trauma, and sociocultural factors, to name a few.

> *I'm going to give you an example from my climbing career. Many years ago, I had a belayer, with whom I used to do a lot of indoor climbing. At this point, the fear of falling had not really entered my mind. One day close to the top of a route, I went to clip the last quickdraw (below the anchor) and slipped. I ended up 2 metres off the floor. An example of poor belaying, soft catch, yes. Put that down as a one-off incident.*
> *A few months later, with the same belayer, a similar scenario occurred near the top! I fell and ended up 2–3 metres off the floor again; this created trauma in my mind. Every time I climbed with this belayer after that, I would look down to see if he was paying attention and purposely not attempt to push myself.*
> *I should have known better, but this happened a third time, not long after – reaffirming this trauma in my mind. I stopped climbing with him. It took me a very long time to get my confidence back, and now, eight years on, it still occasionally enters my mind.*

It's not just trauma within climbing that may affect your mind in dealing with fear. As mentioned before, it can also be from an experience/scenario unrelated to climbing. This trauma can cause people to be more sensitive to 'switching into threat mode' – also referred to as hyperarousal – an increased sensitivity to a thought or action that can induce higher levels of anxiety. Trauma can affect your mind's processing and how it deals with certain scenarios. This combination of the feeling of fear, and the production of adrenaline and cortisol, where the mind tends to focus on one thing at a time, will mean that change may take longer than in someone who does not carry trauma.

In order to create change, we need to work at a level of arousal (discussed in Chapter 3 – comfort zone and risk zone) that we can personally deal with, repeating this process over time, however small these first steps may be. Any change is considered progress, whether this is becoming aware of a behavioural pattern, delaying an old script, or putting in the smallest of changes. Here we need patience, positive affirmation (see Chapter 6 – The Influence of Thought), and support and encouragement from close friends.

THE POWER OF PRACTICE

Neuroplasticity is the term used to describe our brain's ability to adapt to changes. Meaning new neural pathways can be laid down, creating new habits (scripts). The mind is adaptive and will respond to environmental changes. This is how we are able to learn new skills, memorise information, and even recover after a traumatic brain injury. The process of practice in changing behaviours is key. As the Yogis would say, "yoga is 99% practice and 1% theory".

Kevin Karaca on 'Hargreaves' Original' (VS 4c), Stanage
Luca Celano

In 1991, Anders Ericsson, a Swedish psychologist, went on the hunt for talent. After some time searching, he realised he could not find natural talent. Matthew Syed also points out in his book "Bounce" the importance of practice and the myth of talent. None of us are born with it.

When we watch talent shows, we see someone with "talent". But we fail to see the hours and hours of practice they put in, even child prodigies. Take Mozart, for example; by the age of 6, he had put in 3,500 hours of practice. Richard Williams used to take his young children Venus and Serena to the local tennis court to hit a shopping trolley full of tennis balls to practice. Tiger Woods used to watch his dad hitting golf balls for hours and hours in his garage. All the athletes we see in the Olympics have dedicated hours, days, weeks, months, years to the sport they perform in. Your head game in climbing is exactly the same.

We can teach our Pre-frontal Cortex (PFC) not to find useful our Amygdala's reaction in certain climbing situations through practice. Don't feel helpless in your pursuit of climbing; you can change. You need to create the opportunity to do so and put in lots and lots of practice.

Just remember, as mentioned before, to start creating change, firstly start to work within your comfort zone (see Chapter 3), and slowly build this up over time. BE PATIENT!!

"I can't see a way through," said the boy,
"Can you see the next step?" asked the horse
"Yes" said the boy
"Just take that" replied the horse
CHARLIE MACKESY – FROM THE BOOK;
'THE BOY, THE MOLE, THE FOX AND THE HORSE'

Bellavista on Cima Ovest di Lavaredo – 8b+/8c
Thomas Senf

“

I WAS SO SCARED AND DISTRACTED ON BELLAVISTA. FOCUSING ON CLIMBING BECAME DIFFICULT, AS MY MIND FOCUSED ON FALLING. IT FELT TERRIFYING BEING SO HIGH UP.

CLIMBING IS OFTEN A MENTAL CHALLENGE; WORKING ON YOUR INNER FEAR AND OVERCOMING PERSONAL OBSTACLES. WE SEARCH FOR THOSE CHALLENGES, YET WE FEAR THEM AT THE SAME TIME. EXPERIENCING FEAR HELPS US GET BETTER AT CLIMBING. ACCEPTANCE OF THOSE FEELINGS, AND FOCUSING ON THE MOVEMENT CAN BE TOUGH AT TIMES. IN A MOMENT OF FEAR, HOW WE PERCEIVE RISK IS FAR BIGGER THAN THE REALITY. THE ONLY WAY FOR ME TO GET BETTER IS TO FACE THE CHALLENGE, AND ACCEPT BEING SCARED.

”

BABSI ZANGERL

Matt Pickles on Groove Train (33, 8c) – Taipan Wall
Kamil Sustiak

CHAPTER 3

The Learning Zone Model and Optimal Performance Theory

"Change is the end result of all true learning."

LEO BUSCAGLIA

Lizzie is in her twenties and very keen to learn. She has a high-powered job and has always achieved through hard work and persistence. She took up climbing a few months ago as a way of exercise and destressing.

Lizzie has been top rope climbing and wants to progress. She has booked herself on a learn-to-lead course. Today she is attending the third session, where students look at belay techniques to catch falls and falling itself. When it is her turn to have a go, she climbs elegantly. Three-quarters of the way up, the last clipped quickdraw is by her feet. When the instructor asked her to let go, she becomes fear-ridden and grips the holds with all of her might. "Why can't I let go!" Lizzie thinks. The instructor repeatedly, with a calm tone, asks her to let go, to no avail.

The instructor becomes a little agitated and uses a stronger voice, "Lizzie, just let go!". Lizzie does not register the instructor's voice and manages to hold on. With her forearms feeling pumped, she seems to have lost the sensation of how hard she is holding on. With her arms tired, no clear vision of how to escape the situation, she accepts her fate, lets go, and falls off. Pumped full of adrenaline and cortisol, she tells the instructor she wants to come down. She feels disappointed with her performance.

As climbers, we all operate at different levels of comfort and performance in certain situations. We know that we would like to grow what we feel comfortable with and increase the level of excitement we can handle. We know this will depend on our feelings, self-perception, experiences, and any trauma we may carry. We know that many other factors influence this and that it is a very different process from person to person.

How do we make the change needed to stretch our comfort zone and grow no matter where we are operating? Let's first talk about Tom Senninger's theory of the learning zone model, which allows us to identify our comfort zone, and a useful tool for stretching/growing this zone.

THE LEARNING ZONE MODEL

Most of you have probably heard of the 'learning zone model'. It is a model that describes our comfort zone, our learning (growth) zone, and the risk (or panic) zone. The theory suggests that when an individual is placed in a stressful situation (learning/stretch zone), they will respond by overcoming fear and grow as a person.

The model is useful in the sense that within climbing one route we may experience all three zones. If we are then able to identify which section of the activity (i.e. fear of falling, working out the movement on the crux, etc.) lies where on the model, we then have the tools to work on these specific areas to grow our comfort zone, and develop as a climber.

To know which zone you are operating in, the following diagram (diagram 3.1) describes how you may be feeling in each of the zones.

Comfort zone – consists of easy climbing with no stress involved, like your warm-up routes. For Lizzie, this may be climbing routes on top rope, within her physical ability.

Learning zone – this is where you feel excited and exhilarated, and the climbing feels like a challenge; this is where you experience flow (explained in Chapter 4) and where you are exposed to a manageable amount of stress within the challenge. Your skills match the level of challenge, whether this is physical or psychological. Lizzie's learning zone can be climbing at her physical limit on top rope, as well as climbing very easy routes on lead, where there is no potential for her to fall.

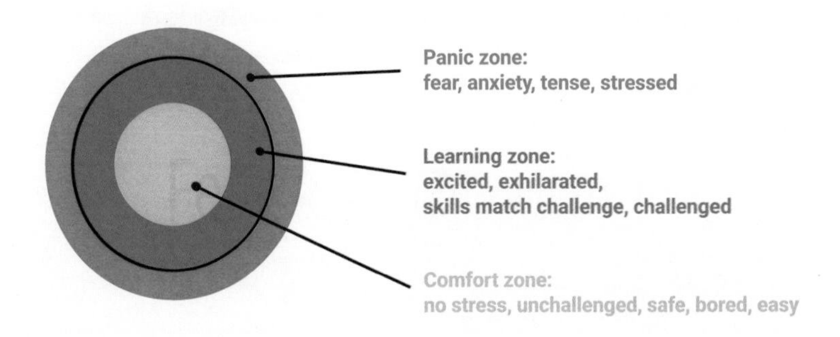

Diagram 3.1 The learning zone model and the feelings associated with each section

Panic zone – this is where you experience fear, feelings of anxiety, and become stressed. You do not climb efficiently here, as you will be tense, doubting yourself, and the single focus can become fear, depending on how far into the panic zone you move.

Move too far outside the comfort zone, past the learning zone, into the panic zone, and stress may be too much for the mind to cope with. The opposite effect will take place, and no positive learning. Moving into the panic zone may even cause trauma, depending on how far you travel into the risk zone. Take our previous example of Lizzie.

Important to remember with this theory is the perception of risk. It is based on how we judge risk in our minds, whether this is real or not. If we perceive something as a risk in the moment – whether this has real consequences or not – we still experience the same physiological and psychological reactions. Like Lizzie, who felt entirely outside of her comfort zone taking her first fall on lead, but we, as the reader, know there are no real consequences to her situation.

If we as human beings operate in the learning zone, we can grow as a person. This is achieved by moving from the comfort zone into the learning zone, before going too far, into the risk zone, where only a small amount of 'manageable' stress is involved. The yogis refer to it as 'leaning into the edge', not past it. Again, the amount of manageable stress is very personal/individual, and sometimes a lot to take on board when knowingly putting yourself into this situation. I guess this is why you have picked up this book; to understand yourself more in a climbing situation and help you develop and progress as a climber. Later on in the book, we will talk about coping strategies (Chapter 10) which will help you deal with the possible stress and anxieties involved in working around the learning zone.

The sizes of the different zones are dependent on each individual; see diagram (diagram 3.2) below as examples.

Ben, has been climbing for five years and can climb 6c-6c+. He doesn't like falling off and avoids it by downclimbing, shouting 'take', or gently lowering his weight onto the rope. Once he has had a rest, he may repeat the process till he gets to the top.

In the comfort zone, we are happy to operate with little to no stress. This feels safe after a while and may even feel boring. If we only operate within our comfort zone, we may not progress, or our progress may result in smaller changes over longer periods of time.

Every time Ben is on an insecure move, where there is the potential to fall, his friends try to encourage him to go for the move. But fear kicks in, and Ben feels he is unable to manage this.

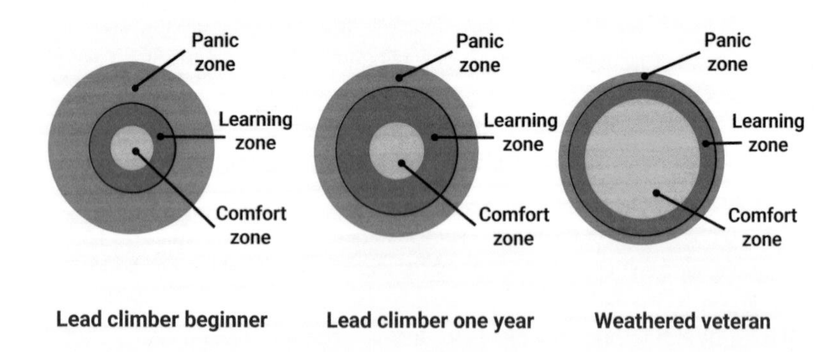

Diagram 3.2 Examples of what the learning zone model could look like for a beginner lead climber, someone who has been lead climbing for one year, and a veteran climber. These are only an example representation, and are not a true representation for each and every individual.

Tonsai beach, Ao Nang, Thailand
Hu Chen

Depending on how far into the learning zone you are operating, it will be stressful/exciting to varying degrees. If we go too far, towards or into the risk zone, we may become paralysed with fear, freeze or even traumatise our brains. Look at the effect it had on Lizzie; taking her first fall on lead was too much for her. To make progress, you need to start becoming very self-aware and knowing where the edge of your comfort/learning zone lies; this can be done through lots of reflection and analysis of yourself after each climb. Be honest with yourself, and prevent from comparing to others (Chapter 6 – The Influence of Thought).

I know there will be those reading this that are very driven and would like instant or quick results. Patience is key here; progress may happen a little at a time, like the careful pruning of a Bonsai tree. If you are unsure about where the edge of your comfort zone lies, start easy, and work your way closer to the edge. Again, BE PATIENT!! As if a Venus Flytrap awaiting its fortnightly meal.

Exercise 3.1, opposite, is a start for you and gives you topics you can work on. If you are unsure where to place the topics, go climbing and try them out. Try to analyse how you feel. The topics in the learning zone, are topics for you to work on currently. The items in the low-risk (panic) zone are things you can work on at some point in the near future, as long as purposeful practice is regularly undertaken. Anything in the high-risk zone may be something to look at again in a few years, depending on your progress you make and the practice you put in.

In climbing, most of us operate within our comfort zones. What we perceive as comfort varies from person to person and depends on our personal experiences. For most of us, our first experience of climbing felt outside of our comfort zone, so why does this feel comfortable (taking away the falling part).

When we move onto the fringe of our comfort zone, where ever this may be, into the learning zone and edge towards the panic zone (not into panic zone), this is where most of the learning happens. So, we need to find this edge within us and operate there to grow our comfort zone. But only in manageable chunks. When we bite off too much, we will revert to our comfort zone or potentially traumatise ourselves.

For instance, the first time you stand at the top of a ski slope, accidentally having taken the chair lift up to the red slopes as a beginner. Skiing down may cause you to give it up there and then – if you make it!

As Ben, from our previous example, climbs above his last clipped quickdraw and is on an insecure move, he realises he may fall off. He freezes, reverts to his comfort zone because this is where he feels safe, and downclimbs.

How do we change this?

HOW DO WE GROW OUR COMFORT ZONE?

Firstly, as mentioned above, we need to be able to identify what topic fits in which zone within our climbing. Once we are able to distinguish these, we have a framework we can use as a starting point. Again, these may change over time, as your comfort and learning zones grow, so be flexible in your approach. Also note that your state of mind and overall well-being may cause these to feel different on different days.

EXERCISE 3.1

Write all of the topics within your climbing in the appropriate area onto the diagram below. If something is a little scary but manageable, write this in the learning zone. If the fear is just outside the manageable zone, place it in the low-risk (panic) zone. If, you currently see no way how you could ever do this, put it in the high-risk (panic) zone. Add the topics you wrote down at the end of the first chapter.

Below are some examples of topics you can use. Feel free to add your own.

Climbing slabs *Bouldering* *Friends watching you climb*

Climbing above a clip, on insecure move

Climbing above a clip *Strangers watching you climb*

Climbing overhangs *Making a clip* *Climbing above an overhang*

Falling above clip, when going to clip next

Top rope climbing *High move on boulder*

Using insecure holds *Falling at a clip* *Falling below a clip*

Being belayed by someone with ATC or non-assisted braking device

Falling from above a clip *Being high up on a route*

Lead climbing *New belayer* *Dynamically moving*

Comfort Zone	Learning Zone
Low Risk (Panic) Zone	**High Risk (Panic) Zone**

The following are steps we can take to grow our comfort zone:

1. Become self-aware of your limits
2. Increase your comfort zone by manageable steps into the learning zone
3. Repeat step 2 until it feels comfortable
4. Move onto the next step, and repeat previous steps

We need to cultivate courage and a self-awareness of our personal limits, a place of vulnerability, excitement and possibly fear at the same time. Self-analysis of your feelings before, during, and after each climb may differ at times, depending on how you feel. Learn to know your boundaries and become self-aware.

> There once was a criminal who had committed a crime
> (Because that's what criminals do. That's their job!)
> Anyway, he was sent to the king for his punishment.
> The king told him he had a choice of two punishments.
> He could be hung by a rope.
> Or take what's behind the big, dark, scary, mysterious iron door.
> The criminal quickly decided on the rope.
> As the noose was being slipped on him, he turned to the king and asked:
> "By the way, out of curiosity, what's behind that door?"
> The king laughed and said:
> "You know, it's funny, I offer everyone the same choice, and nearly everyone picks the rope."
> "So," said the criminal, "Tell me. What's behind the door? I mean, obviously, I won't tell anyone," he said, pointing to the noose around his neck.
> The king paused then answered:
> "Freedom, but it seems most people are so afraid of the unknown that they immediately take the rope."
>
> *Story from book "How to be Happy' by Karen Salmansohn*

Moral of the story is that people tend to choose what they know and possibly feel more comfortable with over the unknown.

To make changes to our comfort zone, we need to have the desire to want to make changes. And, I'm guessing because you picked this book up, that you do. We need to knowingly place ourselves in a situation that will induce some form of excitement/stress, and it may feel uncomfortable at first. With practice, this will get easier over time. We need to work around the edge of our comfort zone

Kevin Karaca on 'Hargreaves' Original' (VS, 4c), Stanage
Luca Celano

moving into the learning zone (refer to the topics in the exercise you completed in the previous section), as long as it is manageable, small steps at a time. Your mind will let you know when you are ready to move on. Instead of going straight for the learning zone, work within the comfort zone and slowly work your way up (please see Chapter 11 – on progressive exercises).

In Lizzie's story, the instructor could have used progressive exercises, allowing her to become accustomed to falling gradually – building up confidence in the system, belayer, and herself.

By overcoming these feelings of anxiety and self-doubt, we can increase our comfort zone and grow as individuals. Like the first time Tony Hawk stood at the top of the big vert ramp ready to drop in; Napoleon Bonaparte's first battle under his command; or the first time you sat on your bike without stabilisers.

Here is an example that may be familiar. Jesse struggles to climb harder routes above an overhang because of the uncertainty of being able to climb it combined with the potential of falling. She could climb lots of easier routes over overhangs (referring to indoor climbing). When she feels it is less scary (only she will know), she can climb a harder route on an overhang. Maybe she can climb up to the overhang – and do this as many times as she needs to until it becomes easier. Then when she feels ready, she can try one move over the overhang. Build her confidence up over time. Then, two moves; only she will know when she is ready to move on.

There are limiting factors that can prevent your progress. One of which is comparing to others. Who cares that Jesse's friend can climb that route. It is only climbing, not the end of the world. No-one really cares what grade/route you climb; only you do. When you do climb it, there will be many more routes and grades to get obsessed with. Jesse has to make sure she does not compare herself to her friend (see Chapter 6 – The Influence of Thought), as this will negate any progress she makes.

To grow our comfort zone, we need to adhere to the following key points:

1. Graded exposure – Taking manageable steps, these are very personal; however small these may be, any change is change.
2. Purposeful training – you will need focused and specific practice with lots of repetition, as stated in the previous chapter. To create change, we need to repeat the process potentially 100's of times.
3. Good support network – to have a supportive group of climbing partners and friends can help here. Feel that you can be open and honest with your struggles, as I bet you, they probably struggle with similar feelings or may have experienced them as well.
4. Be patient and only move on when comfortable with the previous step – There will be some personalities out there that will want to move on quickly, but if you step too far into the risk zone without having become accustomed to the previous steps, you will likely regress, and take a few steps backwards. The ego can be the culprit here.
5. Sometimes, take a few steps back and make sure you don't always operate on the edge of the comfort/risk zone, as this can be emotionally very tiring. Make sure you have fun when climbing, and take off the pressure. It is only climbing and is meant to be a fun pastime.

Sometimes we can see climbers, who have pushed their limits a little too far, clearly in a state of stress. Fighting their way out of panic by scrabbling mindlessly upwards, missing clips (quickdraws), poor foot and hand placements, no communication with the belayer, or no clear plan – this, although progress upwards, is not to be mistaken with mindful 'graded exposure' to fear.

OPTIMAL PERFORMANCE THEORY

Yerkes and Dodson state an optimal relationship between performance and arousal (stress), given a particular task (see diagram 3.3). *"Anxiety improves performance until a certain optimum level of arousal has been reached. Beyond that point, performance deteriorates as higher levels of anxiety are attained."* One may even experience a state called "flow" when at optimal performance (see Chapter 4 – Normal Zone and Flow Zone). Obviously, this differs from task to task and person to person. One person may need a higher level of arousal to perform better given a certain task. Someone else may need a lower level of arousal to inspire higher performance; otherwise, their performance will deteriorate.

If we take a climber who will happily fall off on top rope but not on lead, we can assume that going straight into lead climbing may be too much outside the climber's comfort zone. Here the climber is under some form of arousal but performing well on top rope. Moving to lead climbing increases arousal, this may be by a small/moderate amount, but the drop in performance is significant.

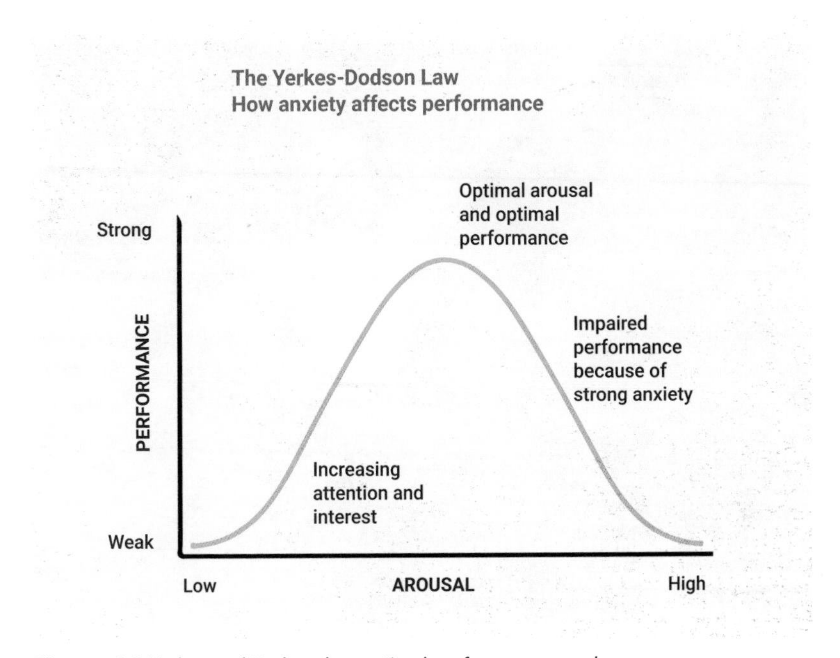

Diagram 3.3 Yerkes and Dodson law optimal performance graph

So we can assume that for this climber the learning zone is on top rope, and their optimal state of performance, according to the Yerkes and Dodson model.

We need to look at the amount of stress/arousal they can handle. Let's say, when lead climbing, every time they clip around shoulder height, it's just like climbing a top rope. The climber becomes very stressed as they climb above this quickdraw until they clip the next one. So, that's where the edge of their learning zone lies. Lots of falling practice needs to be done on top rope, and slowly built up from here (see Chapter 11 – Falling Exercises).

Research has found that different tasks require different levels of arousal for optimal performance. This depends on the complexity, familiarity and difficulty of the task. A certain amount of stress helps us focus, but too much and performance will deteriorate. So, an unfamiliar task may require lower levels of arousal to facilitate concentration and optimal performance. On the other hand, a more familiar task may require a higher level of arousal to induce higher performance. It is very important that you become aware of how much stress you experience within the different aspects in climbing, allowing you to analyse where your optimal performance lies for each given task.

Ben Clark on 'Heading the Shot' (7a+), Seamstress Slab, Serengeti
📷 Luca Celano

CATASTROPHE MODEL

Some people feel that Yerkes and Dodson's U-shaped optimal performance graph (see diagram 3.3) needs to be revised, as it does not consider other variables. Compared to the optimal performance theory, Hardy and Fazey (1988) looked at a third parameter that could affect performance, cognitive anxiety. By cognitive anxiety, they mean the internal anxiety within a person relating to their thoughts and beliefs about themselves and their ideas. Cognitive anxiety refers to expectations, perception, and interpretation of an event, which could produce anxiety (i.e., worry). Diagram 3.4 takes on a wave-like shape; I will try and explain the meaning of the graph.

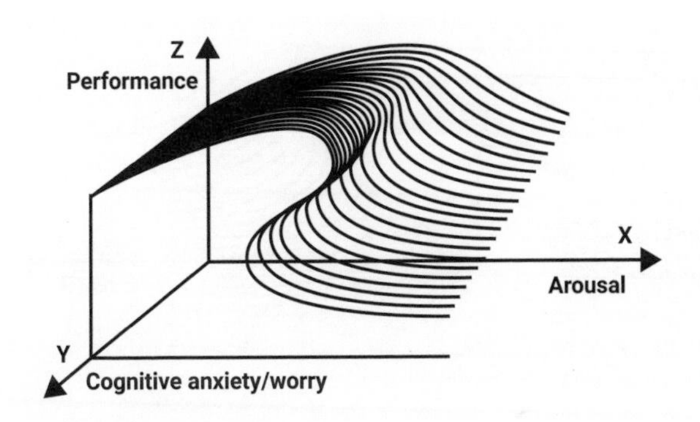

Diagram 3.4 Hardy and Fazey's catastrophe model

Hardy and Fazey's catastrophe model suggests that cognitive anxiety positively influences performance when physiological arousal is low but negatively influences performance when arousal is high. So, at low levels of anxiety, the graph takes on a U-shape, as in the Yerkes and Dodson performance graph (see diagram 3.3, and diagram 3.5 indicated by the yellow line). Conversely, when cognitive anxiety (worry) is high, even a small increase in physiological arousal can result in a catastrophic drop in performance once the optimal performance level is exceeded (see diagram 3.7).

Suppose we take the previous example of Jesse, who struggles to climb harder routes over overhangs with the potential of falling off. She would like to feel ok climbing overhanging routes, so she forces herself to climb them. Even before she sets off, she worries about her performance, expects herself to fail, and believes that she cannot climb overhangs. As she starts to climb, her anxiety levels rise higher and higher as she gains height. She finally arrives at the overhang, debilitated by anxiety, and the idea of climbing another move feels impossible. Her performance drastically plummeted as the optimal arousal levels were exceeded for the level of worry she experienced (see diagram 3.7).

Low-level worry

If you are experiencing a low level of anxiety, as discussed previously, the catastrophe model will take on a U-shape, as Yerkes and Dodson suggest. You will get to the optimal level of performance with a certain level of arousal. If arousal is pushed beyond optimal levels, performance decreases slowly (see diagram 3.5, indicated by the yellow line).

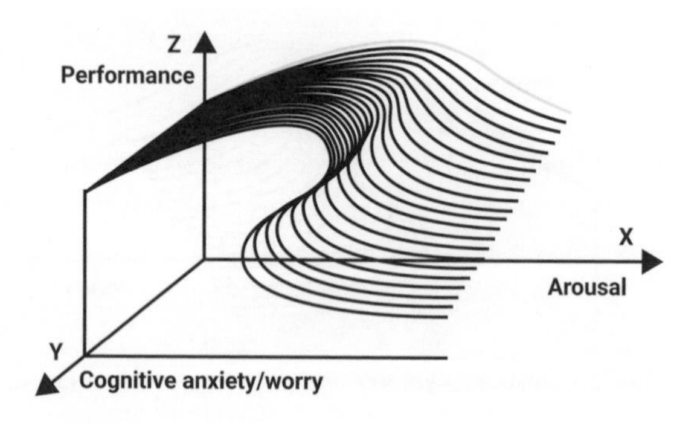

Diagram 3.5 Hardy and Fazey's catastrophe model – low level of worry

Eric Bissell on Tufa King Pumped at Iannis, Kalymnos
Kieran Duncan

Medium-level worry

If you are experiencing a medium level of anxiety, you will get to the optimal level of performance with a certain level of arousal. If arousal is pushed beyond optimal levels, performance will decrease more rapidly than in diagram 3.5 (see diagram 3.6, indicated by the green line).

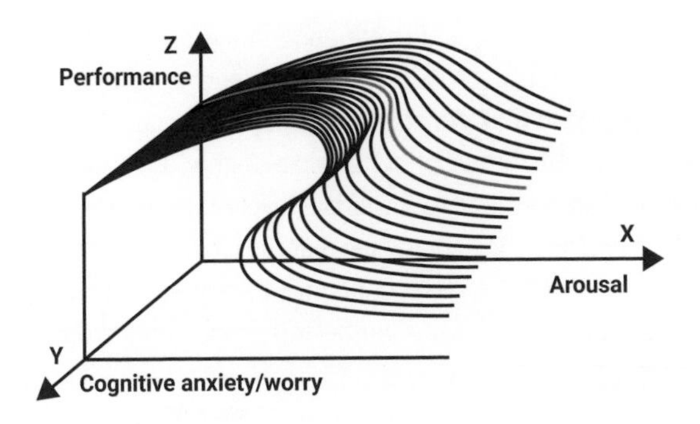

Diagram 3.6 Hardy and Fazey's catastrophe model – medium level of worry

High-level worry

If you are experiencing a high level of anxiety, you will get to the optimal level of performance with a certain level of arousal. If arousal is pushed beyond optimal levels, this will result in a catastrophic drop in performance (see diagram 3.7, indicated by the orange line), just like surfing the top of the wave, pushing too hard, and you'd fall off.

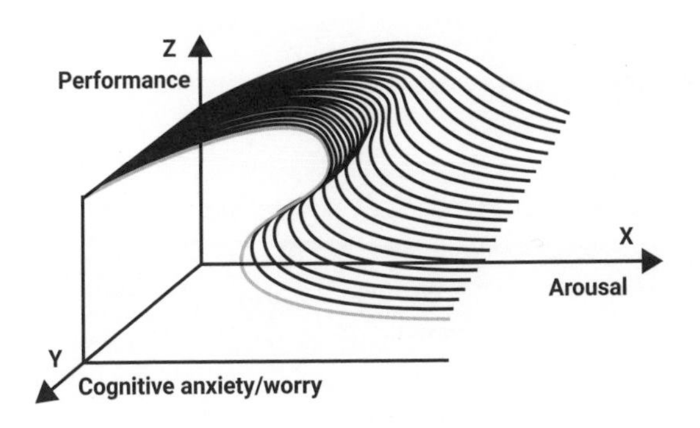

Diagram 3.7 Hardy and Fazey's catastrophe model – high level of worry

This theory states that when someone experiences medium to high levels of anxiety, one will experience a dramatic decline in performance past a certain level of arousal. So how do we explain this sudden drop in performance? Certain anxiety levels can activate the autonomic nervous system, particularly the sympathetic nervous system (see Chapter 1 – Fear and the Brain), which is in charge of our fight-flight-freeze responses.

So, when we are climbing and experience this moment of going too far, our performance drops dramatically. How can we recover from that performance? We need to understand that; we are not our performance. Things happen within us for a reason, and it's the understanding of this that means we can start making changes. So, we need to lower the level of arousal to a point where we will see a rise in performance again (see diagram 3.8). The first arrow indicates a sudden drop in performance, the second show we need to reduce the amount of arousal to a manageable level, before performance can increase again, shown by the third arrow.

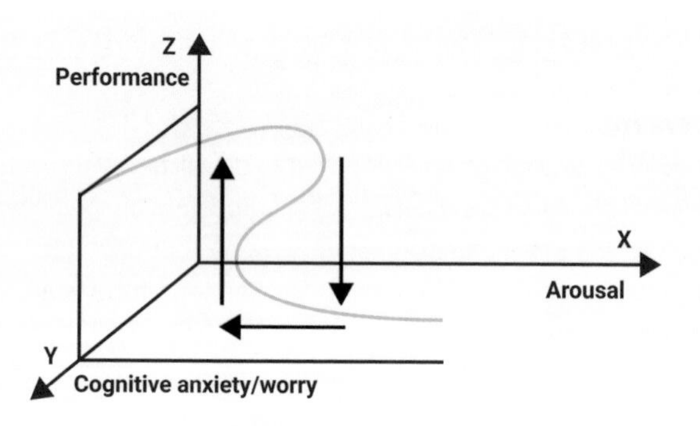

Diagram 3.8 Hardy and Fazey's catastrophe model – returning back to optimal level after catastrophe

We need to create awareness and see how far we can push ourselves to keep our performance at an optimal level, but not too far. Just be aware that this can differ depending on how we feel. Be aware that some people may feel emotionally drained by this dramatic performance drop. So be kind to yourself, and take some time to allow homeostasis (a state of internal balance) in the body and mind before having another attempt. Both visualisation (see Chapter 13 – Performance Anxiety) and breathing (see Chapter 8 – Breathing) can help here to relax and allow the cortisol to be flushed away from your body.

INDIVIDUAL ZONE OF OPTIMAL FUNCTIONING THEORY

Russian-born sport psychologist Yuri L. Hanin, developed a theory looking at the individual differences between athletes, regarding optimal performance. The Individual Zone of Optimal Functioning (IZOF) theory explains that some athletes perform best when they have low levels of arousal, some with moderate arousal, and others when highly aroused. Referred to as being "in the zone".
The theory accounts for individual differences in how we react to arousal and state anxiety (i.e., is the anxiety felt in a given situation). Anxiety can be viewed as a negative, but it can also be deemed to affect performance positively. Therefore, each person has his/her own preferred level of anxiety that allows them to perform at their best.

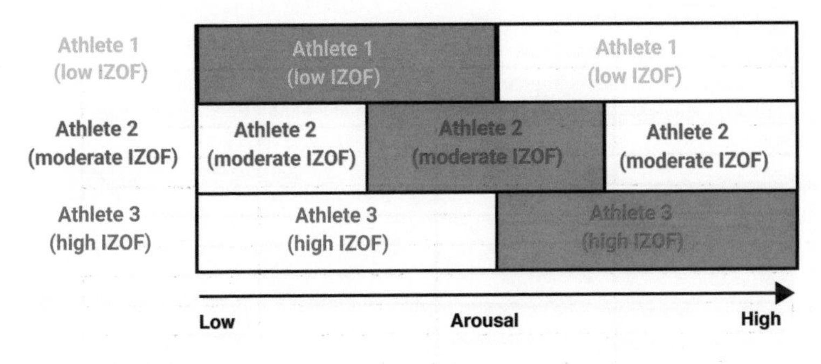

Diagram 3.9 Hanin's Individual Zone of Optimal Functioning theory model

The IZOF theory also allows for a variety of emotional states to be described as helpful or unhelpful in one's performance. For example, for some people, the feeling of excitement may not be beneficial to their performance. Others may find the emotion of anger helpful to reach optimal performance.

So, how do we know where you fit on Hanin's IZOF model? This is where building self-awareness can come in handy. Put yourself in different situations, and notice how you feel, and note how you perform. Record this information (on a notepad) so you have a reference point for next time. Try different climbing situations (terrain, pressures, social aspects, etc.) to see if performance is different. Maybe you need lower/higher arousal levels given certain situations to perform at your best.

We can also use something called individual emotion profiling. Regarding Hanin's theory of IZOF, Emotion profiling is looking at your own individual emotions and how these affect your performance positively or negatively so that you can create a better understanding of helpful and harmful emotions.

An emotion is a physical reaction resulting from either an external influence or an internal experience associated with memory.

According to Debbie Hampton (author of the book *Beat Depression and Anxiety by Changing Your Brain*), "Emotions are lower level responses occurring in the subcortical regions of the brain, the amygdala, and the ventromedial prefrontal cortices, creating biochemical reactions in your body altering your physical state."

They precede feelings and are more instinctual and physical in scope. For example, the first time you go climbing, you may have an instinctual reaction to being at height, resulting in the emotion of fear.

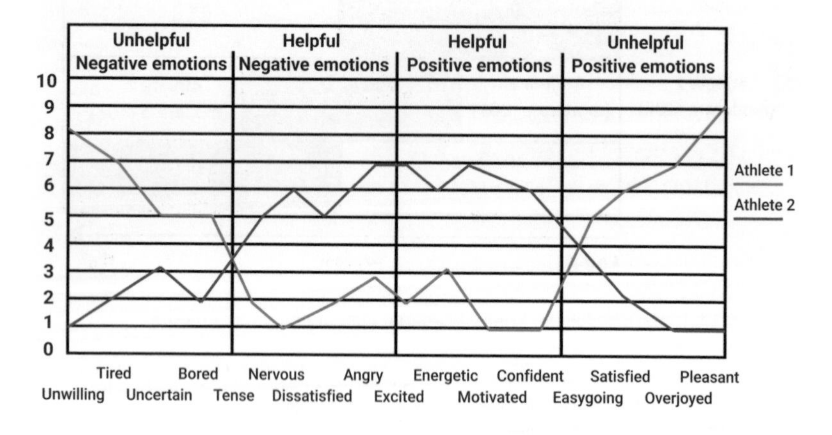

Diagram 3.10 Hanin's Individual Zone of Optimal Functioning theory – Emotion intensity graph

Diagram 3.10 is an example of an emotion profiling graph. It shows a helpful and unhelpful emotions profile for 2 different athletes (iceberg – athlete 1 and cavity – athlete 2). Represented on the graph are positive and negative emotions; some are helpful (cause you to perform better), and others are unhelpful (which are harmful to performance or cause poor performance).

We can see in Diagram 3.10 that there are two plotted lines; one looks like an iceberg, where the unhelpful emotions score lower than the helpful emotions. However, if we look at the red line, we can assume it looks like a cavity, where the unhelpful emotions score higher than the helpful emotions. This performance would really suffer. In an ideal situation, you would like the helpful emotions to score higher than the unhelpful ones for a given performance.

EXERCISE 3.2 – EMOTION PROFILING

The diagram below is a list of negative and positive emotions which can affect your performance. These are just a few examples to get you started. There has been space left for you to **add some of your own**. Once you have added some of your own emotions to the table, which you think have an effect on your performance, please **distinguish** the ones which are **helpful** (cause you to **perform better**), and **unhelpful** (which are **harmful to performance** or cause poor performance), by marking a H (helpful) or U (Unhelpful) behind each **emotion**.

NOTE: Do not assume that a negative emotion will have a negative impact on your performance. For example, nervous and angry are considered negative emotions and may have a positive effect on performance for some people. But also, do not assume a positive emotion has a positive impact on your performance, i.e., for me, excitement and optimism do not always positively impact my performance.

Negative emotions:

Nervous	Bored	Angry
Tense	Uncertain	Frustrated
Tired	Stressed	Jealous
Sad	Failure	Resentment
Overwhelmed	Inadequate	Scared

Positive emotions:

Excited	Motivated	Energetic
Confident	Well rested	Optimistic
Joyful	Happy	Self-collected
Hopeful	Calm	Inspired

Pick 4 emotions to fit in each of the following categories which have the greatest importance or effect on your performance:

Unhelpful negative
Unhelpful positive
Helpful negative
Helpful positive

and add these to the columns below.

The focus is either on pre-performance emotions or on repeated experiences across several performances with similar outcomes. This may take some playing around with and some time to finetune.

Unhelpful Negative	Helpful Negative	Helpful Positive	Unhelpful Positive

Completing the diagram will help you build a form of self-awareness and figure out what emotions are helpful and unhelpful in achieving optimal performance.

Once you have completed the previous table, add these to the Emotion Profiling table below. Make sure these correspond with the correct description (i.e., unhelpful negative, helpful negative, helpful positive, and unhelpful positive).

	Emotion	0	1	2	3	4	5	6	7	8	9	10
Unhelpful Negative	 1	☐	☐	☐	☐	☐	☐	☐	☐	☐	☐	☐
	 2	☐	☐	☐	☐	☐	☐	☐	☐	☐	☐	☐
	 3	☐	☐	☐	☐	☐	☐	☐	☐	☐	☐	☐
	 4	☐	☐	☐	☐	☐	☐	☐	☐	☐	☐	☐
Helpful Negative	 5	☐	☐	☐	☐	☐	☐	☐	☐	☐	☐	☐
	 6	☐	☐	☐	☐	☐	☐	☐	☐	☐	☐	☐
	 7	☐	☐	☐	☐	☐	☐	☐	☐	☐	☐	☐
	 8	☐	☐	☐	☐	☐	☐	☐	☐	☐	☐	☐
Unhelpful Positive	 9	☐	☐	☐	☐	☐	☐	☐	☐	☐	☐	☐
	 10	☐	☐	☐	☐	☐	☐	☐	☐	☐	☐	☐
	 11	☐	☐	☐	☐	☐	☐	☐	☐	☐	☐	☐
	 12	☐	☐	☐	☐	☐	☐	☐	☐	☐	☐	☐
Helpful Positive	 13	☐	☐	☐	☐	☐	☐	☐	☐	☐	☐	☐
	 14	☐	☐	☐	☐	☐	☐	☐	☐	☐	☐	☐
	 15	☐	☐	☐	☐	☐	☐	☐	☐	☐	☐	☐
	 16	☐	☐	☐	☐	☐	☐	☐	☐	☐	☐	☐

On the table, rate how intensive each of these emotions felt prior to a successful or unsuccessful performance, using a 0–10 scale (0 = no effect, 10 = maximal effect). See Diagram 3.11 to add these topics to the emotion intensity graph, to give yourself a physical representation of your emotion profiling. Be sure to add the emotions you have chosen to the lower axis.

As mentioned before, this table will look very different for each individual. It accounts for a limited influence of factors referred to as arousal. It can be hard to quantify these, but completing the emotion profiling exercise will help you better understand yourself. Also, the level of optimal performance can change from day-to-day, performance to performance. It helps to become self-aware, and notice how you perform in each situation, and note what affects it.

	Unhelpful Negative emotions	Helpful Negative emotions	Helpful Positive emotions	Unhelpful Positive emotions
10				
9				
8				
7				
6				
5				
4				
3				
2				
1				
0				

Diagram 3.11 Hanin's Individual Zone of Optimal Functioning theory – Blank emotion intensity graph

Once you have practised completing the table in lots of different scenarios, you will start to gain an understanding of your performance and bring some form of self-awareness to your sessions. Hopefully, you can provide yourself with the best platform to succeed.

Angus Harrison-Smart on Baden Mit Und Ohne, 7a, at Palionisos, Kalymnos
Kieran Duncan

FACTORS THAT CAN AFFECT PERFORMANCE

Let's try and think about the factors that can affect climbing performance or your state of mind; this is important to know, as these can affect the drive to want to make changes and differ for everyone. It is important to know so that we can try to control as many of these as possible to put ourselves in the best possible situation for success. This list could be endless and is very individual. Anything from what you ate last night, to how your relationship is, the daily stresses in life, your mood, how sensitive you're feeling that day, or for women, your emotional and physical wellbeing before/during/after the menstrual cycle.

Another element that may affect performance is your perception of self, which can vary from day to day, or become set within your mind and can significantly influence your expectations or performance outcomes. Even the association we have with arousal, as stated by the Yerkes-Dodson model – how the feeling of butterflies, sweaty palms, and a racing heartbeat can be perceived pre-climb – may induce a sense of doubt in one own's ability. The feeling of arousal before a climb is very normal, and this is where a pre-climb routine can help greatly (Chapter 13 – Performance Anxiety).

These are only a few, and it is well worth noting how you perform and know what affects you in a positive way. When you don't feel the drive to work on pushing your comfort zone, remember that these days will happen – let it go, and have fun. Save working on growing your comfort zone for your better days.

CAN THE COMFORT ZONE SHRINK?

As I mentioned previously, for the comfort zone to grow, we need to perform purposeful practice. By this I mean, practice that requires engagement from the individual, operation in the learning zone and also repetition. The question is can the comfort zone shrink?

If we do not practice something for a long time, e.g., expose ourselves to falling within climbing, our comfort zone may contract. We may have worked on feeling comfortable with falling from above a quickdraw and are now unable to climb for a period of time. Don't be surprised that your comfort zone may shrink. Having said that, with a little practice, the comfort zone will adapt quicker, depending on how much practice has been put in previously, and how you work as an individual. From my own experience, if I haven't had a chance to fall off for a while, on my first session back on the ropes, I will need to fall off to build up my confidence again.

Without purposeful practice, any small improvements we made on top may be lost. So, we are in charge of our ongoing development and need to look at continuous improvements.

> *Sam went climbing last week. He tried to lead climb his first 6b, unbeknownst to him, the belayer was not paying attention. Sam fell off at the top of the route and ended up near the ground. When he next tries to lead climb on a 6a, his anxiety levels are through the roof, and he cannot climb past halfway. In this situation, trauma has affected some of his scripts and his perception of risk. Here, Sam could play around on a top rope till he feels he can get his confidence back before going back into lead climbing and looking at progressive falling exercises (see Chapter 11 – Falling Exercises).*

Whether we witness a climbing accident happening, are involved in a climbing accident ourselves, or step too far into our risk (panic) zone, this will have an adverse effect on our comfort zone. If consequently, we end up with trauma in our brains, we can make changes and progress, but we need to be very PATIENT with ourselves (see Chapter 2 – Scripts and Behavioural Patterns – section on trauma) by taking very SMALL STEPS and lots of repetition.

Also, it is very important not comparing current performance with what you were previously able to do following a traumatic event. If your brain has stored an event as traumatic and you feel it is affecting your performance, take that as a new starting block.

The ego, our sense of self-esteem, self-importance, and personal identity could also have adverse effects on our performance and cause us to edge past our learning zone into the panic zone – Inviting trauma or reinforcing unhelpful scripts along the way. It is important not to put too much pressure on ourselves to perform because of our self-image or our friends' achievements. As mentioned before, it is very important to look at *your* performance and build it up.

REVERSAL THEORY

The reversal theory (Kerr 1987) shows the relationship between our motivational state and sports performance – explaining that we can feel high levels of arousal as both positive and negative depending on our motivational state. Meaning for a given level of arousal, i.e., butterflies, racing heart, sweaty palms, we could perceive this positively, as excitement and ready to shoot into action. Or negatively, as anxiety and in turn affecting our performance. Meaning our motivational state can change the curve of the optimal performance theory.

It could be as simple as rephrasing how we perceive arousal. But as the research here is limited and incomplete on how we can control our motivational states, I will not delve further into this theory. But it is useful to know and be aware of how we may perceive arousal, especially in chapter 11, where we look at progressive falling exercises.

CONCLUSION

The Learning zone model is a tool that helps us identify the comfort zone in order to enable change. The Yerkes-Dodson optimal performance theory and the catastrophe model state that we can grow as individuals, given a particular task, by introducing a manageable amount of stress/excitement. Just keep in mind that each individual operates at their best, given different levels of arousal (IZOF theory). So, for optimal learning to occur the mind has to be able to cope with the stress/arousal induced. It needs to be at a manageable level, and also different enough to create change.

Our measure of success, as a climber, should be on creating change in our comfort zone and the learning process. Everything else is a bonus. Our main aim should not be completing a route or getting to the top; these are mere additional outcomes from hard work. Our main focus should be the learning process. Be courageous, and learn to move into the learning zone with graded exposure. Be vulnerable with yourself, and set aside your ego. Continue your development and change your routine regularly to avoid stagnation.

Big Bang – 9a, Lower Pen Trwyn, North Wales
Marc Langley

“

CLIMBING THE BIG BANG DIDN'T JUST HAPPEN OVERNIGHT. THIS ROUTE TESTED THE LIMIT OF MY PHYSICAL AND MENTAL CAPABILITIES, IT REALLY PUSHED MY SELF-BELIEF SYSTEM.

I DREW ON ALL MY KNOWLEDGE TO ACHIEVE SUCCESS, I SET MYSELF OTHER GOALS FOR CONFIDENCE BOOSTS THAT I COULD ACHIEVE RELATIVELY QUICKLY. I HAD ROUTINES AND RITUALS THAT WERE TAILORED TO ME BUT THE TWO BIGGEST THINGS THAT MADE A DIFFERENCE TO ME WERE MAKING SURE I TOOK A POSITIVE AWAY FROM EACH SESSION (EASIER SAID THAN DONE SOMETIMES) AND USING VISUALIZATION TO THE POINT I WAS DREAMING ABOUT CLIMBING THE ROUTE JUST BEFORE I DID IT. I NEVER GAVE UP BELIEVING THAT I COULD DO THIS ROUTE AND USED MY STUBBORNNESS AS A STRENGTH, I PUSHED MYSELF BEYOND WHAT I BELIEVED I COULD ACHIEVE BY TAKING A RISK ON A DREAM GOAL, IT OPENED MY EYES UP TO THE POSSIBILITY OF MORE, WHICH IS ALWAYS EXCITING.

”

EMMA TWYFORD

Amandine Loury on La Ligne Claire (8c),
Saint Léger, France
Damien Largeron

CHAPTER 4

Normal Zone and Flow Zone

"Most enjoyable activities are not natural; they demand an effort that initially one is reluctant to make. But once the interaction starts to provide feedback to the person's skills, it usually begins to be intrinsically rewarding."

MIHALY CSIKSZENTMIHALYI

I approach Cairn Lochan, full of nerves, anticipation, and anxiety. Having completed a pre-climb ritual of not talking, sorting out the gear and rope, setting up a belay, I replenish from the 2-hour approach with a swig of water and a frozen snack bar. I then set off on my adventure upwards. Fear dissipates and is replaced with such singular focus that the rest of the rockface could have fallen, and I would not have noticed. Every movement made with such resolute attention; there is no turning back; the only way is up.

Clearing the built-up rime from the surface of the 400-million-year-old granite is like a builder removing old plaster from the walls. Finding imperfections to hook with my ice axes, small crystals became gigantic boulders. I weld my protection into every crevice I can find, and inch my way up the slightly overhanging rockface. Breathing heavily with burning calves and cold hands, none of this registers in my conscious brain. I'm too focused on the now. Everything flows and makes sense. Topping out feels like an intense release of pressure and I'm overcome with a feeling of elation. I let out a euphoric bellow. I look at my watch and realise I have been on the route for 5 hours. How is that possible? It feels like I only just set off.

Have you ever climbed a route where every movement flowed, no stress was involved, and the climbing felt effortless? You reached the top, but once down, you struggle to remember how you climbed the route; this is what some sports psychologists refer to as the flow zone. The flow zone is when your subconscious takes over and climbs for you. All distractions disappear, and all of your attention is focused on your performance, resulting in quicker reactions, faster processing of information, and increased energy efficiency. I will try and explain in this chapter just what this means and how you can achieve it.

NORMAL VS FLOW ZONE

Normal Zone

Let's first talk about the "normal" zone where our prefrontal cortex is engaged, the thinking part of our brain. The prefrontal cortex is responsible for higher cognitive functions, like distinguishing right from wrong, planning our social behaviour, decision making, connecting with our working memory, and self-expression.

We spend most of our everyday lives, from the moment we get up to the moment we go to sleep, in the "normal zone"; from planning our day, deciding what to cook for dinner, our interactions with other people, the thoughts that move through our brains at any given time, and so much more. These thoughts can sometimes feel like distractions, especially when we try to focus on one task. In our busy lives, we sometimes struggle to turn off this internal dialogue.

Flow Zone

The flow state, or being in the zone, is a state where you are so involved in an activity that nothing else seems to matter. Attention is solely focused on the task at hand and all sense of self and time seem to disappear; all that matters is the moment itself. It is an advantageous and therapeutic state of mind to achieve as we feel good about ourselves, achieve incredible personal goals, learn more about ourselves, and create a sense of contentment along with a rush of happiness.

So, where does this state of being come from, and how do we get there?

THEORY OF FLOW

In the 1960s, Mihály Csíkszentmihályi, a Hungarian-American psychologist, was the first to describe the concept of 'flow'. Steven Kotler, a flow researcher/author and director of the Flow Genome Project furthered this research. Looking into ultimate human performance, he further developed the concept of flow and advanced research around the subject.

As stated by Mihály Csíkszentmihályi, *"The best moments usually occur when a person's body or mind is stretched to its limits in a voluntary effort to accomplish something difficult and worthwhile. Challenges expand ourselves. Such experiences are not necessarily pleasant at the time."*

In this state of 'flow', people are completely absorbed in the activity, using their creative abilities to their utmost; this is where you feel strong, alert, effortless, fearless, confident, and unaware of yourself. That all sounds great, so how do we get there?

Andrew Finney on 'Shorty's Dyno' (6c+), Above the Rails, Australia
Luca Celano

CONDITIONS FOR FLOW

Triggers

We now know what flow is, but how do we get there? What triggers it? According to Csíkszentmihályi's theory of flow, ten components will trigger and move you into 'flow'. These are:

- **Clear goals** – as a climber, these may be climbing a route without falling, flashing your first 6b route, climbing with perfect technique, being able to work out the 'climbing puzzle', etc. ... As a climber, you may not always be aware of 'clear' goals, but the intention is to climb and get to the top or see how far you can climb.
- **Immediate feedback** – when we are climbing, we continually receive feedback through our senses: does the hold feel good, am I in balance, do I need to shift my centre of gravity, am I relaxed or pumped?
- **Concentration** – we need to be concentrating on the task at hand and each movement as it comes up. Our concentration will be disturbed if the challenge level is too high for our abilities, or the challenge level is too low, and our thoughts are elsewhere – we may end up in a state of boredom.
- **Sense of control** – the feeling of exercising control in difficult situations; hence you need to challenge yourself the right amount. In climbing this means you must climb at, or near, your physical or psychological limit throughout some, or all, of the climb.
- **Loss of self-consciousness** – happens when a task is entirely engrossing, and all attention is in the moment. There is no room for other thinking; it is a balance between skill and challenge; this is where, momentarily, the 'self' (ego) or awareness of self disappears.
- **Distorted sense of time** – this is where all sense of time is lost. Time may appear to move faster or slower.
- **Balance between skill level and challenge** – as mentioned before, you need to challenge your skill level, whether physically or mentally. Please see the next section for further information.
- **The activity we partake in is intrinsically rewarding** – within climbing, there are several aspects. Overcoming a particular challenge, whether physically or mentally, hanging out with friends, the climbing movement itself, being outside in nature, and many more.

Unknown climber in Lvíčka, Karlovice, Czechia
Petr Slováček

- **Engrossment in activity** – this goes hand in hand with focused concentration on the task at hand, where everything else disappears, and all of life's worries fade away.
- **Unaware of bodily needs** – as we become so engrossed in the moment, we forget about being hungry, thirsty, tired, etc.

When we look at the above list, we can see that climbing can tick many, if not all, of the above boxes most of the time. According to Csíkszentmihályi's theory, the three main components are: clear goals, immediate feedback, and the challenge/skill ratio.

Let's take a more detailed look at balancing skills vs challenge ratio.

SKILLS VS CHALLENGE

It is a fine balance between skill vs challenge, and something that can be easily overlooked. The following diagram has been taken from Mihály Csíkszentmihályi's book, *"Flow: the psychology of optimal experience"*.

Every time you climb, you will end up somewhere on this diagram, depending on the relationship between your skills and how challenging the climb is. As you guessed, you want to be on the flow channel, matching your personal skills to the challenge at hand.

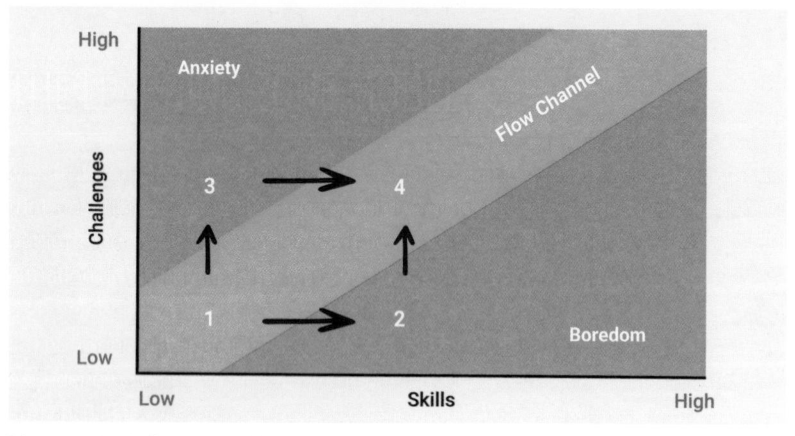

Diagram 4.1 Csíkszentmihályi's flow diagram

Csíkszentmihályi uses the example of a tennis player. As this is a book for climbers, let's use the example of climbing.

> *Sam, who has been climbing for one year, has just learned to sport lead climb. He can climb some 6b routes. He has just managed to get his head around clipping the rope into the quickdraws but struggles to clip when he is above the previous quickdraw, especially on an insecure hold/move.*

There are two issues here; clipping above a quickdraw and being on an insecure move/hold.

1. Sam has decided to look at clipping above a quickdraw first. He has decided to practice this on 6a and 6a+ routes. Whenever he is above a clip, going

for the next one, he is in flow, matching his skill level with the right amount of challenge.

2. A few weeks go by; Sam feels a little bored by now. He is comfortably climbing all 6a's and 6a+'s without any trouble. Here, climbing 6a+'s isn't enough of a challenge, and this is where boredom kicks in; this is where the challenge becomes lower than the skill level. Instead of experiencing flow, Sam experiences boredom.
3. Alternatively, Sam does not like practice and can be impatient. He decides to climb 6b's on lead and does not feel the need to practice clipping on 6a+'s. Whenever he gets above a quickdraw, on an insecure move, he freaks out, is overcome with fear, and decides to downclimb until the previous clip is around head height.
4. Neither boredom nor anxiety is a positive experience. So, glancing at the diagram, for Sam to return to flow from number 2's situation, he needs to climb 6b's as this is where his skill level will match the challenge, and he will be reintroduced to the state of flow.

If, on the other hand, Sam finds himself at number 3 on the diagram, he has pushed himself too hard too soon and finds the levels of anxiety are too much to handle.

He can lower the challenge by climbing more 6a's and 6a+'s until he feels it is becoming boring and then increase the challenge to 6b, where he will move back into the flow channel.

From diagram 4.1, we can derive that we need the right amount of challenge to match our skills to arrive in a state of flow. We need realistic goals, and these differ from person to person. Flow state is reached just 4% outside of our comfort zone.

THE SCIENCE OF FLOW

What happens physiologically when we get into flow? Through Steven Kotler's research and the Flow Genome Project, we now know what happens in the body and the sequence of events that occur.

Let's take the previous example of Sam, who has practiced climbing on lots of 6a+'s, and cruises to the top every time with little effort but is yet to climb a 6b. As he approaches the first-ever 6b attempt (we know that his skills match the challenge), he feels nervous; the body is pumping cortisol (stress hormone) around, and internally he is getting ready for the fight-or-flight response. Here is where Sam can act in two different ways; either climb (fight) or move to an easier climb (flight). Either of these is a normal response. Both can feel very overpowering to some.

The feeling of excitement and stress can almost feel the same, and the same chemicals are involved in the process; adrenaline and cortisol.

In this case, Sam decides to climb. He focuses on a few deep breaths (Chapter 8 – Breathing; and Chapter 13 – Performance Anxiety), moving into acceptance (of what is to come) and the relaxation response.

Nitric oxide enters the bloodstream and flushes away the fight-or-flight chemicals.

Sam starts to climb; as he enters the state of "flow", his body produces 5 of the most powerful natural chemicals. These are;

- Norepinephrine (also known as noradrenaline) – increases heart rate; reduces the size of blood vessels, in turn increasing blood pressure; increases blood sugars, so we have more energy; it also increases arousal, alertness and focuses our attention.
- Dopamine – is associated as a reward chemical and can produce feelings of euphoria. A boost of dopamine will cause you to feel more alert, increase focus, reduce mental noise, increase blood flow, and increase motor control. Steven Kotler refers to it as a 'skills booster'.
- Anandamide – the happy chemical which gets released with physical exercise; a pain reliever, it increases lateral thinking (creative thinking), and very importantly, it inhibits the potential to feel fear.
- Endorphins – these reduce pain and increase the feeling of pleasure.
- Serotonin – is responsible for feeling happier, being more focused, feeling calmer, and less anxious.

Flow is one of the only times when the brain is flooded with all of these chemicals at once.

In the right circumstances during climbing, we can see the benefits of each of them. They are all very potent reward chemicals. Steven Kotler compares the above naturally occurring chemicals and, with the exception of one, illicit drugs.

Dopamine – Cocaine
Norepinephrine – Speed
Endorphins – Heroin
Serotonin – Prozac
Anandamide – Marijuana

Alex Oates competing in the Winter Comp at the Warehouse Climbing Centre
Mike Chrimes

To give you a comparison and a perspective of their potency, you can see why the state of flow can become very addictive. Hence, people use the term 'adrenaline junkie'.

The brain is 2% of body mass and uses 20% of the energy from the body. Conscious processing (prefrontal cortex) is very slow and energy-consuming, whereas sub-conscious processing is quick and energy-efficient. During flow, sub-conscious processing takes over, and parts of the brain shut down – all mental noise disappears.

Arne Dietrich, a psychology professor at the American University of Beirut, refers to it as transient hypofrontality. Let's break it down: transient = temporary, hypo = to deactivate or slow down (opposite of hyper), frontality = pre-frontal cortex.

In transient hypofrontality, we are trading conscious processing for subconscious processing. Information is processed very quickly, requires little energy, and cuts out mental noise; this results in quicker reactions and increased productivity.

What's not to like about faster processing using less energy? Albert Dijksterhuis, a Dutch social psychologist, ran an experiment in 2009, where he asked a group of football experts to predict the outcome of a selection of matches. One group was given 2 minutes to analyse the statistics and any variables they think could influence the results to predict the matches' outcomes. The second group was given the same conditions, but they were distracted with a complicated memory task.

The second group outperformed the first, better predicting the results of the matches. The first group's conscious processing got in the way; they were overthinking. The second group's subconscious predicted the results, whilst the memory task occupied their consciousness.

When in 'flow,' the prefrontal cortex becomes less active, as does the amygdala, which is at the centre of decoding stressful stimuli; this is all fantastic while it lasts, but what happens if you get scared and lose the feeling of flow?

MOVING IN AND OUT OF FLOW

When we are climbing, we may be in a flow state. If we then end up on an insecure move above a quickdraw, we may become conscious of our position and begin to focus on the possibility of falling off. This might sound familiar; we start to over-grip (see Chapter 7 – Pumped Forearms), our breaths become shorter (Chapter 8 – Breathing), and our primary focus becomes the possibility of falling off. No other thought is penetrating our conscious mind; the stress is too much as we have entered too far into our risk zone (Chapter 3), and we revert to our comfort zone by following the scripts (Chapter 2) we have set within our brain. We do this by downclimbing and shouting "Take" (as an example). When operating between flow and the fight-or-flight response, all it takes is one negative thought to send us in a downward spiral.

This is where breathing comes into its own (see Chapter 8 – Breathing).

Additionally, if you feel too much adrenaline (also known as epinephrine), it means you are feeling too much fear and should be looking to lower the challenge level. You may benefit from progressive falling exercises (chapter 11 – Falling Exercises). It is essential to match your skill level with the challenge you set yourself. As mentioned before, it is also beneficial to operate just on the edge of your comfort zone, in the learning zone, where you deal with a 'manageable' amount of adrenaline.

Leonidio, Greece
Fionn Claydon

FINAL WORD

To find the right level of challenge for you, moving into flow, and trusting yourself, takes a great deal of practice (well-structured practice), as well as self-analysis, knowing your limits, and lots of hard work. We also need to embrace failure (see Chapter 5 – Failure and the Growth Mindset). Only through our willingness to fail do we accept ourselves and can grow.

Vail World Cup 2018

Angie Payne

“

OVER THE YEARS ONE OF THE BIGGEST THINGS I’VE LEARNED IS THAT IT’S IMPORTANT TO TRAIN YOUR MIND AS MUCH AS YOU TRAIN YOUR BODY. CLIMBING IS DIFFICULT AND CONSTANTLY PRESENTS NEW CHALLENGES, SO IT’S IMPORTANT TO STAY POSITIVE AND ALWAYS BELIEVE IN YOURSELF!

”

MEAGAN MARTIN

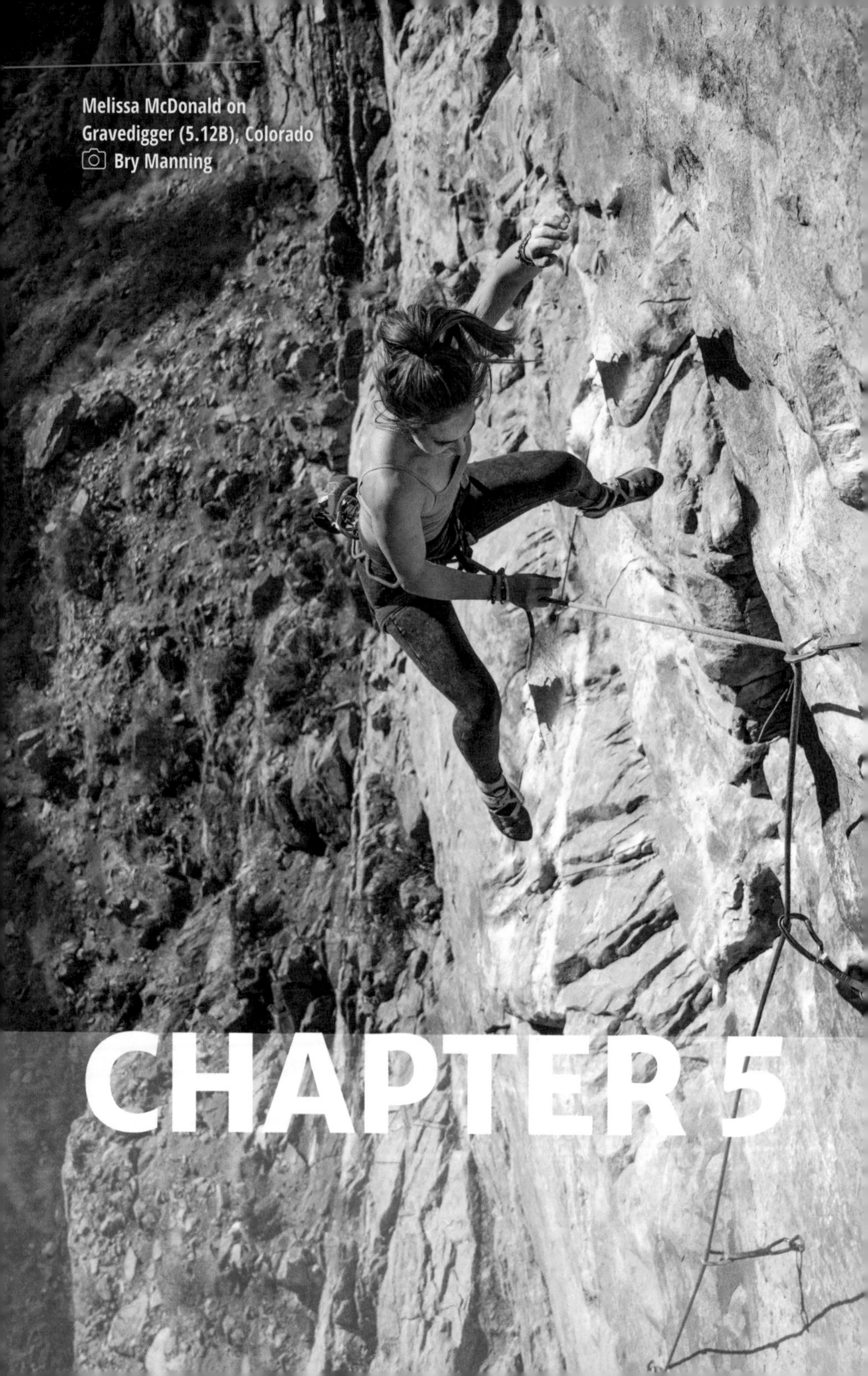
Melissa McDonald on Gravedigger (5.12B), Colorado
Bry Manning

CHAPTER 5

Failure and the Growth Mindset

"Success is not final; failure is not fatal:
it is the courage to continue that counts."

WINSTON CHURCHILL

In 1996, the year eBay started its online auction, two old foes battled for supremacy for 120 gruelling nail-biting minutes in the European Championship semi-final. England was playing Germany at Wembley, fighting for possession and every inch of domination on the pitch. After a 1–1 draw and a 6–5 penalty shoot-out, it was Gareth Southgate's turn. Cheered on by an anxious onlooking crowd, Gareth set off on that lonely walk from the centre circle. He places the ball on the 12-yard penalty spot. A darkness came over him from the realisation that the world is watching. The German goalkeeper seemed to have grown in the last few moments as he lines up to take his shot.

Gareth runs forward, his eyes locked on the ball, like a hawk targeting its prey as if his life depended on this single moment. His body is perfectly lined up to canon the ball into the top corner. However, the pressure was too much, and he mishits the ball straight into the arms of Andreas Köpke, the German goalkeeper. Momentarily, his world collapsed around him; he has a gut-wrenching realisation that it is all over. Gareth's fear of failure got the better of him.

If you look at my climbing career, I have failed more times than I have succeeded. I have been unable to achieve some significant objectives, as well as smaller ones. I have been benighted on routes (unplanned bivouac), lowered off as fear became too high. I've gotten lost, not had the right climbing partner, or just not had the energy or experience to continue.

Ben Roberts on 'Remain in Light' (6c), Yellow Wall, Serengeti
Luca Celano

WHAT IS THE FEAR OF FAILURE?

Fear of failure is the fear of not completing or succeeding in a task or action. This fear can be so overpowering that it prevents many from even attempting a task. It is a form of self-sabotage or procrastination and affects people in many different ways. A small percentage of people are consciously aware of this, but most are unaware. The fear of failure could be a subconsciously deep-rooted fear stemming from childhood due to having overly critical parents. Perhaps a high-pressure educational system causes anxiety where we are expected to complete tests and get labelled as low, medium or high achieving. Sometimes bullying or a traumatic event may have caused a long lasting skewed view of oneself. Fear can also be self-inflicted due to personality traits or social pressure.

The causes mentioned above can stem from deep-rooted scripts, schemas, and habits set within all of us. Nowadays, social media's influence does not help the situation, with perfect air-brushed images and the perception of ideal lives that do not truly reflect real life's struggle.

The feelings associated with the fear of failure are low self-worth, uncertainty, shame, or embarrassment. People who fear failure will not attempt a task if they 'THINK' they may fail; they are protecting themselves from this feeling of shame and unworthiness.

You may also have the perfectionist who is driving him/herself to achieve at the highest level; they put an excessive amount of pressure on themselves to succeed, which in itself can promote anxiety. As they do not want to fail, the perfectionists' focus is on the end result instead of the learning process.

As we read in chapter one, situations we perceive as dangerous can trigger the threat response. Shame is equally capable of triggering our survival brain into the fight-or-flight response. The sympathetic nervous system is activated. We express ourselves through behavioural aggression (fight), usually towards ourselves, or freezing because we feel trapped and powerless; this causes us to blame ourselves.

Shame is usually associated with people being around us who witness our actions, and we feel judged. We may be conscious of this but mostly unaware. Simplistically put, we want to be socially accepted by our peers, fit in, and not be judged.

> *A perfect example of this can be found in some climbing centres where you may have a core group of strong climbers. They usually hang out there several times a week and are always shouting encouragement to one another. Some may even take off their tops (talking about the boys here) because they feel they can climb harder that way. Another climber comes into the room/space, who is not part of the group, and nine times out of ten would feel intimidated. This other climber would like to have a go at a climb but is aware of being watched by the group; he/she decides to climb out of sight; this is a perfect example of fear of failure, in the form of perceived rejection: the fear of not being accepted or judged by the group.*

This feeling is closely related to our primal, survival-related fear of being socially excluded.

> *Another example would be avoiding a particular route, as you may have to deal with a level of fear with which you are uncomfortable. You do not want to be judged by the belayer, your peers, or the other people around. Showing others that you have a fear of falling can feel very vulnerable.*

If we objectively think about anything we would like to learn or achieve in life, it will involve some form of 'failure'. The first time we picked up a pen and learnt to write in our early childhood took lots of practice and wrist ache to get right. The first time we tried to get on our bike and cycle took numerous attempts to master without the assistance of an adult or older sibling holding the seat to stabilise.

It is the same in climbing, whether you are relatively new to climbing or have been climbing for years. If you are climbing at your personal, physical, or psychological limit, you are 100% certain that you will experience 'failure' at some point. What is a failure but a learning point and challenge for next time. Why do we label it as a failure? We have a tendency, as human beings, to describe and focus on our failings and not the small achievements within what we do.

You may have a grade A student that gets a B for the first time and is mortified. Or someone who appears to be continually 'failing' as the educational system labels them that way – they are never praised for the effort they put in. Consequently, they grow up not making an effort as that is what has been expected of them. Why put energy into something when you feel it will be wasted and not recognised?

To illustrate this, we climb a route and fall off a particular hold. We come back to the ground and confirm that we cannot climb the route as we think we are not strong enough. We use another negative label (see Chapter 6 – The Influence of Thought) and confirm our lack of self-belief. Regardless of what we have achieved up to that point, if we feel ashamed of a particular climb, we may not attempt it again. Why put ourselves through that feeling of embarrassment again?

Without practice we may never achieve our full potential. You may be in a Mexican stand-off. On one side, your fear holds you back; on the other side is the drive to want to achieve. It may feel easier to allow fear to control you, as you will less likely put yourself in a situation where you will feel uncomfortable. As you have picked up this book, I'm assuming you would like to make a difference in how you deal with falling and failure in climbing, and as previously mentioned – we can change! To change, we need to work in the learning zone and use various coping strategies to deal with the situation. As long as you practice and repeat this process as many times as you need to, then change will happen. All of the small changes and learning points will create a growth mindset within you.

Phil Rose competing in the Winter Comp at the Warehouse Climbing Centre
Mike Chrimes

GROWTH MINDSET

What is a growth mindset? It is the knowledge that ability and intelligence can be developed over time.

Carol Dweck, a social psychologist with a keen interest in intelligence theories, believes success results from hard work and learning. *"In a growth mindset, people believe that their most basic abilities can be developed through dedication and hard work – brains and talent are just the starting point. This view creates a love of learning and a resilience that is essential for great accomplishment"* (Dweck, 2015).

Carole Dweck (2006) explains that someone with a fixed mindset believes that ability, intelligence, and character are fixed and do not change over time. By avoiding failure and challenges at all costs, they deceive themselves into feeling intelligent and skilled. Someone who thinks they have a growth mindset, believes that through purposeful practice ability can grow. As Matthew Syed describes the myth of talent and the power of practice in his book *"Bounce"*.

Dweck (2006) ran an experiment where a group of people were divided into two equal groups, dependant on the outcome of a particular test. One group was praised for effort (i.e., growth mindset), whilst the other group were complimented for their intelligence and results (i.e. fixed mindset).

Both groups were then offered a slightly easier or slightly harder test. The fixed mindset group opted for the easier test, as they did not want to underachieve. Whilst the growth mindset group chose the harder of the two tests, as they wanted to challenge themselves.

Unbeknownst to both groups, they had been given the same test difficulty.

The fixed mindset group results showed that they performed worse than in the first test, whereas the growth mindset group performed better.

A fixed mindset can have an incredibly negative impact on the perception of self and our ability. It can be set within us from early childhood, where we are encouraged to achieve results continually; this is especially recognisable in our educational system. Opposite is an illustration depicting the differences in both mindsets.

Both Dweck and Syed talk about the power of purposeful practice, learning, and a growth mindset.

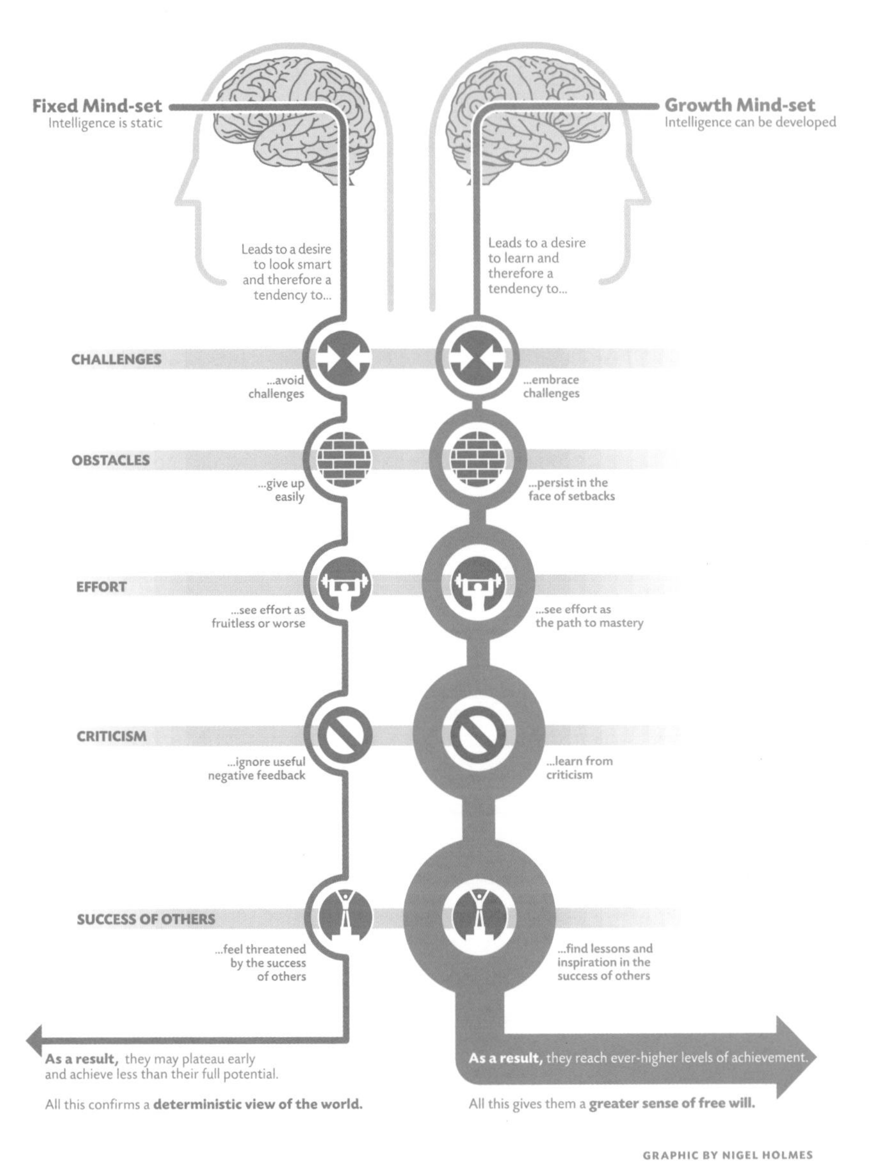

Diagram 5.1 Carole Dweck's two mindsets chart

GROWTH MINDSET'S RELATION TO FAILURE?

As mentioned previously, when tackling a new task, is it reasonable to expect ultimate performance from the get-go? The first time you went swimming, you certainly did not swim 100m on your first lesson unaided. The first time you got into a car to learn to drive, it took a few goes to get the hang of balancing the clutch and the accelerator pedal without stalling?

So why, when it comes to certain climbing situations or other parts of life, do we have such high expectations for our performance? These consisted of all learning points built up over time to produce what we know now.

It is the same with regards to falling in climbing. Why, when we experience fear in the following situation, do we expect ourselves to feel comfortable falling off whilst trying to go for the next move above the last clipped quickdraw? Why not put in lots of purposeful practice regarding falling in climbing and build this up? Or why not take enjoyment in 'failing' your way up a route, and learning how we could climb it in the future.

A growth mindset highlights our relationship with perceived failure. If we climb a route to the point where we feel scared and end up downclimbing because the fear we felt was too intense, it is not a 'failure'. We need to change our perception of 'failure' and ourselves. Just because you have felt this for a long time does not mean we have to live with a fixed mindset. We have already learnt that the brain is malleable and can lay down new neural pathways a little at a time. It just takes a little courage to realise that we can change, accept ourselves for who we are, and not worry when things don't always go to plan (Chapter 6 – The Influence of Thought).

Do you feel anxious when faced with a challenge, or does your head tell you to stay away? Try to observe your reaction when faced with a setback or criticism. Do you try and justify this by way of an excuse? Do you become defensive, angry, or crushed instead of learning from the feedback? Observe when you climb with someone who is 'better' than you within a particular part of the climbing process. Do you feel envious and threatened, or do you feel eager to learn? Accept those thoughts and feelings and work with and through them.

The diagram opposite describes how we may talk to ourselves when we have a fixed mindset. Compare this to the different language we would use if we had a growth mindset.

Diagram 5.2 Fixed and growth mindset

Fixed mindset	Growth mindset
"I can't get over the fear of falling. I'm a failure."	"When I downclimb as a result of fear, I find where the edge of my comfort zone is."
"That's ok, I'm not very good at climbing."	If you catch yourself saying "I will never be able to do that grade." Just add the word "yet" to the end of that sentence.
"Don't worry, you'll get it if you keep trying." – You need to use the correct strategy, and purposeful practice, otherwise your efforts may be lost.	"That feeling of the fear of falling feeling really hard work in the moment, is your brain growing."
"Great effort you tried your best."	"The point is not to get it all right away. The point is to grow your understanding step-by-step. What can you try next time."

EXERCISE 5.1

Can you think of any climbing situation where you use a *fixed mindset* self-talk? Please write these down in the first column. Once you have completed your list, please write how you may change these statements to a growth mindset in the second column.

Fixed mindset statement	Growth mindset statement

WHAT CAN WE DO ABOUT IT?

Adam Ondra did not climb 'Silence' (a 9c route in Flatanger, Norway) the first time. It took him four years and many attempts. Alex Megos did not climb Bibliographie (a 9c route in Céüse in France) on his first attempt. It took him around 60 tries over three years, with lots of specific physical and mental training. Both Adam and Alex struggle with the fear of failure to different extents, but we would not immediately associate this with athletes at their level.

Alex's mindset was that he would not attempt a route if he felt he would never be able to get to the top. Here his focus is getting to the top. But how do you know you can climb something unless you try and work it. Alex realised that he should embrace failure; otherwise, he may never find out whether he has the ability to climb those routes.

Failing can make us feel small, not good enough, and decrease our motivation to push through.

Just remember, failure is part of the journey. The difference between success and not so successful is that successful people don't quit.

Ways to overcome the fear of failure?

- Change our perception of failure – failure is but the realisation of our limit at a specific point in time. It gives us a challenge to work on for next time, whether this 'failure' is physical or psychological. The next time you climb and decide that the fear you experience is too great to manage and escape this uncomfortable feeling by downclimbing – don't consider not climbing the route or not facing the 'danger' as a failure. Think of it as a learning point; this may be too far outside your comfort zone and something to work up to.
- Accept yourself – we live in a world of social media, bombarded with images and video clips of perfection – someone doing something better, or someone somewhere living a better life. These are a skewed reflection of life. Quieten your inner critic, be kind to yourself, and accept where you are. There will always be better, and there will always be worse.
- Focus on the positives – when we climb and fall off our project or fail to continue because fear feels too intense, focus on the positives. Initially, you may find this hard to do, but be persistent, and the results will follow.
- Focus on the learning process – and not the results. Being ego-driven or focusing on results will produce a fixed mindset, create a fear of under-achievement, perpetuate the negative perception of self and your ability.

- Setting goals – setting positively framed goals instead of negatively framed avoidance goals. For example, instead of saying, 'I am going to try and not fall off', you could say, 'I will try and climb and see where I can get to'. Instead of 'I hate falling,' you could say, 'I would like to feel more comfortable with falling".
- Challenge yourself – don't be afraid to 'fail'. Climbing would not be as rewarding if it did not feel like a challenge.
- Bitesize chunks – when challenging yourself, create small manageable challenges, enough to create change but not so much that you become paralysed with fear.
- An encouraging group of friends – to have a great support network around us can be very reassuring. Be sure to express to your friends what helps you perform better and let them know what is not helpful.
- Fear list – write a list with everything you fear in climbing and the worst-case scenario of these fears. This list can help you realise what fears you need to overcome and enable you to track progress over time. You can also write down the benefits of overcoming each of these fears and realise that the advantages far outweigh the fixed mindset.
- Purposely failing – Choose to challenge yourself, knowing you will not be able to complete it. For example, the grade-A student hands in a draft of their assignment, or the climber who stays within their grade, tries a route where they have to climb from clip to clip, resting between. Build up a bank of positive 'fails' instead of shame. Again, make sure you operate in your learning zone and not past it.

By 'failing', we learn a lot. I have learnt more about my 'failures' in climbing than my successes. My 'failings' show me where the edge of my comfort zone is, where I need to learn more, and where I need further purposeful practice. Focus on the learning process, challenge oneself, and the rest will follow. When you get there, there will always be more to learn or harder grades to practice.

Gareth Southgate's England penalty miss was considered a weakness by the masses and himself. He later became the England football coach and worked on getting better at penalties and, in doing so, managed to turn his failure into success. He then took England from being ranked 14th in the world to 4th, further making his initial failure into the entire England football team's success.

Be kind to yourself, have fun, and focus on the process of climbing.

EXERCISE 5.2 – FEAR LIST

In the diagram below, please write down the fears you face when climbing. Please remember this is an exercise in perceived danger, where the consequences must not lead to injury, as these are real fears. Thinking about fear of falling and the fear of failure.

Fears	Worst case scenario	Benefits of overcoming
1		
2		

IFSC combined qualifiers
Toulouse/Tournefeuille 2019
Rémi Fabrègue

> IN 2002, WHEN WE WERE 17 (BASSA) AND 11 (MICKAËL), WE DID NOT HAVE REGULAR ACCESS TO A CLIMBING GYM. WITH LIMITED RESOURCES AVAILABLE TO US, WE FOUND WAYS TO BECOME STRONGER. THROUGH HARD WORK, DETERMINATION AND UNCONVENTIONAL TRAINING METHODS AT THE TIME, WE CLIMBED OUR WAY TO REPRESENT FRANCE. 'THERE ARE NO DREAMS WITHOUT HARD WORK.'

BASSA MAWEM

Jade Ross competing in the Winter Comp at the Warehouse Climbing Centre
📷 Mike Chrimes

CHAPTER 6

Before we start the next chapter, I would like you to complete the following.

Please get a piece of paper and write all of the topics you think would positively or negatively affect your climbing performance.

Close the book and spend around 5–10 minutes on the exercise.

I know some of you will be tempted to read on, but please try this exercise before moving onto the next page.

Once completed, open up to the next page.

There is no right or wrong here. Anything that may affect your climbing performance is very personal. In my experience, when people complete this exercise, very few people write down a topic related to the influence of negative thought. But negative thoughts can have a substantial effect on our performance.

The Influence of Thought

"But if thought corrupts language,
language can also corrupt thought."

GEORGE ORWELL

There was once a very strict monastery following a vow of silence; no one was allowed to speak at all. But there was one exception to this rule. Every ten years, the monks were permitted to speak just two words. After spending his first ten years at the monastery, one monk went to the abbot. "It has been ten years," said the abbot. "What are the two words you would like to speak?"

"Bed... hard..." said the monk.

"I see," replied the abbot.

Ten years later, the monk returned to the abbot's office. "It has been ten more years," said the abbot. "What are the two words you would like to speak?"

"Food... stinks..." said the monk.

"I see," replied the abbot.

Yet another ten years passed. The monk met with the abbot once more; he asked, "What are your two words now, after these ten years?"

"I... quit!" said the monk.

"Well, I can see why," replied the abbot. "All you ever do is complain."

Through our focus on negativity, we can be our own worst enemies.

A Zen story

Ollie, a confident, dark-haired optimist who loves climbing, spends most of his life pursuing achievements and living life to the full. He climbs a route just on the edge of his physical ability, reaches for an insecure move, and feels a little pumped. The little voice inside his head tells him he cannot make the next move, as the hold looks worse than what he's currently on. The only time in his life, doubt gets the better of him. He hesitates and keeps telling himself, "I'm not gonna make it, I'm not gonna make it'. Then out of nowhere, he makes a half-hearted attempt at moving his body up to the next hold but doesn't even make it halfway. His brain had already decided his fate.

But where does this all come from? Why do we sometimes talk negatively to ourselves and judge ourselves so harshly?

We talk to ourselves, not how we would speak to a friend, so why do we do it? That inner critic – from where does it come? Does it stem from parental influence and the way language was negatively used against us? Was it the educational system that pressured all of us to achieve an end goal? Is it society that only seems to put us on a pedestal when we achieve? Is it the bullying we may have experienced as a child? Or is it innate within us all?

I'm afraid I cannot answer this question, but we can change how we perceive ourselves. As mentioned previously, these may be habits (Chapter 2 – Scripts and Behavioural Patterns) set deep within our brain and may take lots of conscious work to change.

Beth Dexter on 'Indian Summer' (6a), Castle Inn Quarry
📷 Luca Celano

THE ROOT OF NEGATIVE THOUGHT

From a young age, we spend a lot of time in an educational system, where the focus is on the end result; tasks, tests, exams, essays, etc., which are all marked against the same standards and criteria. We are then all judged on the mark we achieve against the work we produce.

I think this can be very damaging to an individual. We forget about the learning process and the personal achievements of each person. For example, it may be a bigger achievement for someone who has dyslexia to achieve a grade A (80-90%) than for a straight 'A' student to achieve an A* (90-100%). I'm not saying that the straight 'A' student does not work for it, but thinking about the relative effort it has taken the individual with dyslexia to achieve an A grade.

We move onto the workplace, set projects to complete, tasks to do, and work our way up the promotion ladder. We are critiqued for making small mistakes and are judged and assessed for the work/job we do.

We are rarely praised for small stepping stones in our learning/achievements throughout our formative years. This process of continual affirmation, of 'doing better' and looking at the end-goal, causes us all to lose perspective on the progress we have made and learning to enjoy the process. We project this view on the rest of our lives. Striving becomes a habit and is often driven by fear, perfectionism and a whole host of critical and unhelpful thinking. Eastern philosophies have recognised this trap for hundreds of years. Practices for challenging this way of life have been cultivated in philosophies underpinning health and wellbeing.

> *I'll give you an example from my climbing career. I spent a year and a half training for a big climb. When it came to performing, all went well, but I only managed to get halfway.*
>
> *For me, this was a failure and very emotional as I realised I could not proceed due to injury. I felt like a failure because I had not achieved what I set out to do. After some time went by, I looked back and realised what I had achieved. I had learnt so much up to the point of what we call in western society "failure".*

We often seem to miss the point. What if we concentrated on just the learning process and viewed each step as a small achievement with everything else a by-product of these smaller achievements. Wouldn't that be great?

What is a failure, but a learning point and a challenge for next time?

NEGATIVE SELF-TALK

I'm sure we have all been in the same situation as Ollie. Think about how much negative words can affect you. Words carry energy, just like anything else. If everybody realised how much power words had, they would never speak another negative word about themselves or give power to another negative thought again.

> *As a climbing instructor, I come across this concept a lot. I once had a client who climbed 6c-6c+ mostly, but she wanted to climb 7a. Watching her climb on her first session, I could not see why she could not climb 7a. So, I asked her if she wanted to climb a 7a, she responded with, "I'm not a 7a-climber.". She struggled her way up, did not climb as efficiently, and had a few takes on the crux.*
> *Once down on the ground, after a good rest, I suggested she climbs a 6c (which was actually a 7a but chose not to tell her). She climbed it with little effort and seemed to climb with confidence. She came down and said that it was hard for a 6c. I congratulated her on her first 7a.*

Most of you wouldn't talk to a friend like you do to yourself. Negative self-talk can influence our biochemistry, our state of wellbeing and how we feel. It can cause us to feel fear, anger, anxiety, guilt or shame, to list a few. The effects on our biochemistry include the feeling of weaker muscles, variable or higher stress and hormone levels.

Negative self-talk has been linked with depression and increased mental health problems. Focusing on negative thoughts may also lead to a decrease in motivation and higher levels of stress. None of these helps us in climbing. Horn (2008), Weinberg and Gould (2011) suggest our behaviour and thoughts are directly influenced by our expectations of success. As seen in chapter 5 (Failure and the Growth Mindset), if we focus on grades, we enter a fixed mindset. If we focus on the learning process and the effort we engage with; we encourage a growth mindset. As Carole Dweck (2006) demonstrates in a simple experiment, she ran (please see details in Chapter 5). As mentioned previously, our measure of success should be based on the progress we make in our learning, not just on achieving a particular grade/route.

There are lots of different types of negative self-talk. Opposite is a list of the most commonly recognised thinking patterns (Aaron Beck & David Burns) and some examples from the climbing forum. We all experience negative self-talk, whether it be one form of thinking or a combination of the below-described patterns. Which one do you think you tend to favour?

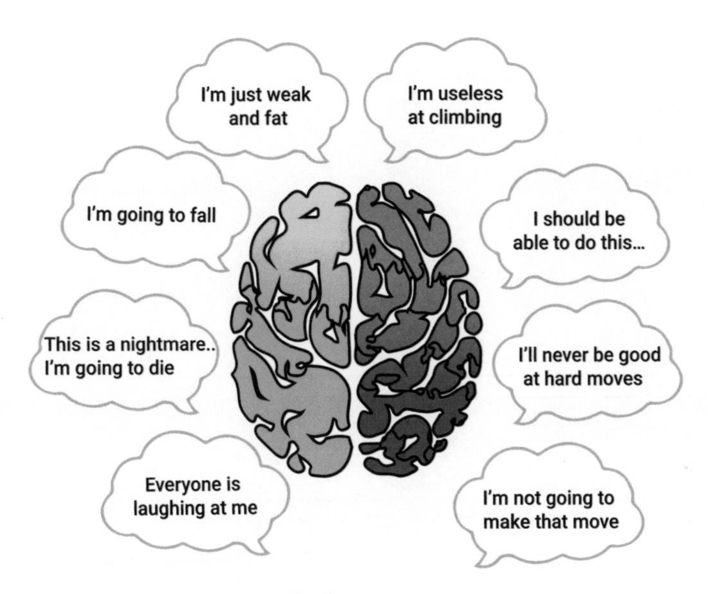

Diagram 6.1 Examples of negative self-talk

Mental filter	
Only noticing what the filter wants him/her to notice. Focusing on the negatives of a situation. Using dark blinkers, gloomy specs or seeing a glass half empty.	**"That move just before the top was clunky and out of flow"** Jenny climbs her project (previously done with three link-ups) with determination and elegance, effortlessly floating until she slips off after the crux. She climbs the remainder to the top. Afterwards, she feels angry and frustrated and focuses on the foot slip only. The rest of her session is affected.

Worrying	
It's normal for humans to worry about future events that may or may not occur. Sometimes this can become an unhelpful habit. Psychologically, we are distracted from the present moment, and the body releases epinephrine (adrenaline), increasing heart rate, breathing, and raising blood sugar. Muscles will tense. These consequences affect climbing efficiency. See chapters on fight/flight processes (Chapter 1), flow states (Chapter 4) and breathing (Chapter 8).	**"I'm going to fall on the next move"**
Self-criticism	
The self-destructive inner saboteur tells us we can't do something, points out 'under performance' and picks holes in personality. Repeating this self-criticism process can have a substantial effect on our self-image, building a self-limiting view of ourselves and a self-fulfilling prophecy. This pursuit of limiting our self-image will have effects on our performance.	**"I am just too heavy and weak-minded!"** We fall off a particular move on a route and focus on what we didn't do and why we could not get any higher. We use negative words to describe what happened. "I'm not strong enough to hold that hold", "I don't have the technique to make that move", "My body is the wrong shape to fit in that space", "The footholds are too small", etc.
Prediction	
Also known as crystal ball gazing is predicting the outcome of what will happen on a future event.	**"I'll get to the overhang and then struggle or fall off"** Predicting when we'll fall off due to fear.

Playing victim	
A form of self-criticism where we compare ourselves negatively to others and feel sorry for ourselves without analysing all of the parameters that may play a role in the situation, e.g. personality, experiences, body makeup, the way we learn.	**"I'm just never going to be any good at it"** "if they can do it, I should be able to… "I'm just hopeless and should not bother anymore."
Labelling	
Describing ourselves or others in an extreme characterisation often based on a single event or behaviour. Through repetition, we believe the label to be accurate and ultimately create a fixed perspective.	**"I am just weak-minded and fearful"** Tom has a fear of falling and reaffirms this to himself every time he gets scared, "I am a fearful climber", and decides to downclimb, as opposed to trying to face his fears.
Memories	
We recall past (often emotional) events. We apply the feeling to the current scenario. These do not have to be associated with similar situations.	**"Last time I felt like this, I looked really stupid in front of everyone."** If we take my example, from chapter 2, where I had nearly hit the floor on three occasions due to bad belaying. Every time I climbed after that, the feelings of high anxiety came flooding back, even with different belayers.
Shoulds and musts	
These types of thoughts put an excessive amount of pressure on oneself and set us up for unrealistic expectations. Often rooted in family or cultural expectations, these are unhelpful and can cause us to feel anxious as a result.	Sophie, the strong static 6b+ climber, tells herself, **"I should be able to climb every 6b"**. With that statement comes the pressure to perform, especially in front of a crowd.

Mind-reading	
Assuming what others are thinking (usually about ourselves) without any good evidence. Derren Brown, the English mentalist and illusionist, may be able to suggest what we are thinking; but ultimately, even with lots of non-verbal signals, most of us are just guessing. Generally, as a climbing community, my experience is that we are all encouraging of one another and try to be helpful if we can.	**"Everyone is laughing at me"** Thinking our belayer thinks we are a scaredy-cat when they are really thinking "What can I do to encourage them.".
Emotional reasoning	
This is where your emotional reaction confirms to you a thought pattern. For example, I feel bad, so I must be bad; I feel anxious, so I must be in danger. We are not our emotions; emotions are a physical representation of what we are thinking or feeling at a particular point in time.	**"I feel embarrassed, and so I should back off as people may laugh"**
Black and white thinking	
Also called splitting or all-or-nothing thinking. We think in complete extremes; either everything is really good or really bad. Ideally, we would like to look at both the positives and the negatives to give us a realistic view; the black, the white, and the grey (the positives, the negatives, and everything in between).	**"If I cannot climb that route, what's the point?"**

Mountains and molehills	
Sometimes referred to as magnification and minimisation. Exaggerating the risk, danger or negatives; minimising the odds of how things are most likely to turn out, or minimising the positives.	Sophie, a strong static 6b+ climber – who occasionally feels the fear of falling getting the better of her – tries to attempt a dynamic 6b techy route. She fails to climb the crux and decides to downclimb and rest on the rope. Instead of seeing this as a one-off, she begins to think, **"This is it – I am NEVER going to be able to climb harder grades; This was a TERRIBLE performance, and I don't think I will ever bother to try again."**
Catastrophising	
Imagining and believing that the worst-case scenario will happen. This almost goes hand in hand with predicting.	**"I'm going to die!"** An example would be thinking you would fall off a route the first time you try it. But how would you know without having tried it?

Jane and Sarah have climbed for three years. They have similar physical strength and ability.
Jane climbs 6c consistently and Sarah around 6b-6b+ but with an occasional 6c. Sarah is very competitive and highly focused on climbing 6c. She thinks she should be climbing the same grade as Jane. When she starts a 6c, she is overwhelmed by her nerves because of the pressure and thought processes that underpin her motivation to try. Even before she leaves the ground, her body is stressed, and this immediately affects her efficiency. Furthermore, every time she falls off, she says to herself, "I am not strong enough and not a 6c climber".
Jane does not care what grade she climbs because she enjoys the process of climbing. She doesn't criticise herself when faced with a potential challenge or call herself names when she fails. She focuses on becoming a better technical climber. This freedom allows her to

enjoy working on a specific technique, sequence of movements, and challenging her head game (unhelpful thoughts are normal after all!). Jane praises herself for small improvements and accepts when she is tired/undermotivated and labels them 'play' sessions.

Wouldn't it be great if we could flick a switch in our brains and switch all of this off and climb in-the-moment?

EXERCISE 6.1

We hardly ever look at our overall performance and focus on the positives. As an exercise, the next time you climb, climb a few routes (below your limit) as best you can, and come up with three things you did well. For example, look at the execution of specific movements/techniques or the way you held a particular tricky hold. Write them in the space below:

How did you get on?

Some of you may not have trouble with this, but I imagine most of you found it hard to name three positives of how you climbed a route(s).
The idea here is to focus on the positives and look at what you see as negatives as a challenge.

Alles is Gut, was Man Gerne Tut (7a+), Frankenjura, Germany
Fionn Claydon

WHAT CAN WE DO?

This is undoubtedly a work in progress. It will take time and patience with yourself. We may find that sometimes we feel very 'stuck' in our heads and preoccupied with intrusive and unhelpful thoughts. The first step is most important: ***becoming aware of our thinking patterns*** and noticing our thoughts 'in the moment'. Following that – cultivating a version of you that talks kindly about personal achievements and successes will help build a better self-image, promoting healthy balanced thinking; this will take patience and acceptance, which most of you will HAVE to practice. Just like climbing, if you do not practice noticing AND changing the way you talk to yourself, things will not improve. Just thinking about it is not enough.

Try practising becoming aware of your thought patterns away from climbing, and slowly bring these into climbing situations. Practice in non-stressful situations first. Accept the days when you feel no progress is being made.

Once we become aware of our thinking patterns, there are many methods we can use to challenge our thinking. Some of the most common are listed below:

- Self-soothing – through the use of breathing techniques, conscious positive affirmation, self-hypnosis (see Chapter 13) **"It's going to be fine."**
- Thought challenging – challenge your 'inner voice', and replace the irrational parts with reasonable, positive statements **"There is no evidence that today I will fall."**
- Thought distracting – through breathing techniques, listening to music, or singing a song. See chapter 10 for different coping strategies which can be used in a climbing situation.
- Problem solving constructively – clarify your problem objectively. Analyse the actual issue from the psychological noise; that way, it can help you grasp the 'obstacle' and help solve it **"if I inhale, prepare, exhale, and reach while pushing off my right foot, I will make it."**
- Self-motivating – find out what motivates you to change your behaviour; a reward (e.g. chocolate bar); the knowledge of change; friends; music; the idea of climbing a higher grade or better, etc. **"Just think how good you will feel for persevering."**

Positive self-talk, in particular, builds self-confidence and changes self-perception and the belief that we can achieve success. Steps can include:

1. Notice the critic inside, and the thought pattern
2. Separate the critic from yourself — observe your thoughts; you are not your thoughts
3. Talk back using one of the methods described above
4. Be in the present – be aware that these negative thoughts are based on past experiences or on future instances that MAY or MAY NOT happen
5. Replace with positive affirmation and constructive thoughts

Remind yourself of small and previous achievements. Start each climb as a new challenge, and don't allow your previous failings to determine who you are. A pre-performance routine can help lower stress and clear the mind (Chapter 13 – Performance Anxiety) before you set off.

Building self-confidence can change our self-perception and the belief that we can achieve success.

As mentioned previously, our measure of success should be based on the progress we make in our learning, not just on achieving a particular grade/route.

However, this can be a by-product of our hard work (Chapter 5 – Failure and the Growth Mindset) and used as motivation.

"The best climber is the one having the most fun."
ALEX LOWE

EXERCISE 6.2

Try and notice some of the thought patterns your mind follows in and outside of climbing situations. Write these in the column below. Analyse which type of thinking this is, and create an alternative thought for each of the examples. They do not have to be climbing related but try to draw on a few different types of responses that have been described. For example, replacing "I am going to fall" with "If I fall, this will be a sign that I am trying hard and making progress".

Thoughts	Which thinking pattern	Replacement
E.g. I am going to fall	*Prediction*	*If I fall, this is a sign that I am trying hard and making progress*

THE INNER GAME WE PLAY

Tim Gallwey, a tennis coach, very quickly in his coaching career saw the importance of learning from images rather than words. As he describes it, he noticed that we all have a Self 1 and a Self 2. Where Self 1 is the teller (or ego), and Self 2 is the doer. Whenever you do something, Self 1 judges what you do, good or bad, hence labelling your performance. Once you label that performance, Self 1 can instruct Self 2 to do it again, perform better, or focus on an element of the performance to get better at. Instead of trusting Self 2 to perform and learn from its own 'successes and failures'.

Judgement begins with labelling performance, which causes interference with one's climbing with a reaction of anger, frustration, or discouragement. Judgemental labels usually lead to emotional reactions and then tightness, trying too hard, self-condemnation. Errors are an important part of the development process. Expectation of performance is also a judgement of what you should be doing, not focusing on the doing and being in the moment.

Self 1's (the ego) mistrust of Self 2 (the doer) causes both the interference called "trying too hard" and that of too much self-instruction. The first results in using too many muscles, the second in mental distraction and lack of

Kopa on Celtic Dragon, 8c+, Illiada, Kalymnos
Kieran Duncan

Leevi Toratti on Honk Down, 7c,
El Chorro, Spain
Kieran Duncan

concentration. Next time you climb, observe how Self 1 can take over before you set off. Or observe Self 1 taking over as you are climbing and getting closer to the point you may struggle. Doubt creeps in with Self 2, resulting in tightening up, frustration, and possibly judgement.

The first skill to learn is the art of letting go of the human inclination to judge ourselves and our performance as either good or bad. The initial act of judgement, good or bad, will start the process of self-instruction, trying too hard. The mind is anything but still, the body's muscles are tight with trying. Letting go of judgements does not mean ignoring errors. It simply means seeing events as they are and not adding value to them. Non-judgemental awareness.

Give yourself a clear visual image of the results desired, which is the most useful method of communicating with Self 2. It is essential to trust Self 2; Self 1 (the ego) must stay relaxed. Self 2 will act and learn without being told or being micro-managed. Let go of judgements, and let natural learning happen with images. Too many instructions interfere with our performance. The more awareness one can bring to your action, the more feedback one gets from the experience, and the more natural learning happens. It is learning how to feel and not judge it.

Putting the mind in the present; that's how you quieten Self 1. Look at Chapter 10 for an array of coping strategies which may help.

CHALLENGE YOURSELF

'Embrace imperfection and challenge yourself.'

This is not the same as driving yourself through self-criticism or threat-based thoughts. Anything that can be looked upon as negative can consciously become a challenge for next time. As an example, there is a particular move on a climb that you keep falling off of.

Instead of falling into the trap of telling yourself you are not strong enough or do not have the technique to climb that sequence, you need to analyse this move and look at how you CAN make the move. Do we need to train and get our fingers stronger or work on a specific technique to make the move? Or is it fear which is holding us back?

If you're struggling to work it out, ask a friend to help or ask a climbing coach/instructor. Challenge yourself to make that one single move; don't worry about the rest of the climb. Use positive affirmation every time you try your challenge. It doesn't matter whether you climb it or not. One day you will.

'A challenge is an opportunity to learn.'

CONCLUSION

Unhelpful thoughts are often the result of habits (scripts) engrained in us. We have ultimately practised BEING this way. So it will take some work to change this and train the brain (via new neural pathways) for quicker routes to more helpful, compassionate and positive thoughts to become a habit. Ultimately you are not your thoughts. Catch yourself when these occur, try and use any one of the coping strategies (Chapter 10 – Coping Strategies) to distract yourself in the act whilst on a climb. Work on accepting yourself for who you are and how you are.

This book can only scratch the surface on this topic. As a climbing instructor, I work with what I observe constructively. Becoming aware of your style of self-talk and other influencing factors can bring up strong emotions. If that happens to you and interferes with your day-to-day life, go to your GP (doctor) to ask about options for trained people to talk to, try finding a compassionate ear amongst the people you know, and talk to friends.

> "Because one believes in oneself, one doesn't try to convince others.
> Because one is content with oneself, one doesn't need others' approval.
> Because one accepts oneself, the world accepts him or her."
> **LAO TZU**

Lary Arce on Kalea Borroca 8b+, Siurana, Spain
Will Smith

IFSC combined qualifiers
Toulouse/Tournefeuille 2019
Rémi Fabrègue

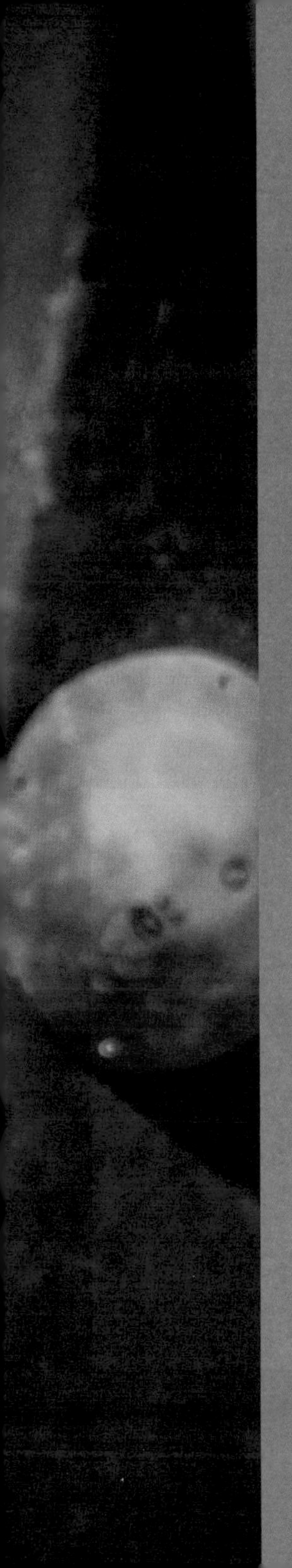

“NEVER GIVE UP, FIGHT ALL THE WAY, KEEP MOVING FORWARD AND NEVER LET A POOR PERFORMANCE DETERMINE WHO YOU ARE. THERE ARE TIMES WHEN THE WILDEST DREAMS SEEM ACHIEVABLE, ONLY IF YOU DARE TO TRY THEM.”

MICKAËL MAWEM

Band Yakhchal, Iran
Omid Armin

CHAPTER 7

Pumped Forearms

"If my mind can conceive it, and my heart can believe it—then I can achieve it."

JESSE JACKSON

The sun is creeping around the edge of the limestone cliff, slowly warming everything in its line of sight. Moving between pockets, crimps, tufas, and some really bad slopey holds, my forearms feel as if they are burning. My anxieties are compounded with the worry of the crux of the route coming up. Beads of sweat rolling down my forehead and breathing in fear, my forearms feel as if they are going to explode. I am losing the sensation of my ability to feel and hold onto the rock. Accepting my fate of falling off, I close my eyes, focus on my breathing and release the tension in my body and hands the best I can. I feel as if I have been there for hours when, in fact, I have only been there moments.

The sooner I fall off, the sooner I can rest my forearms. Let's just have a go. Before I knew it, I clipped the chains. How did this happen? I thought I was completely pumped!?!

I have added a chapter in this book titled pumped forearms because when fear kicks in within climbing, our 'fight/flight' response kicks in. As a result, we may end up squeezing the holds we are on a little harder because we do not want to fall off. Using up that last little bit of energy we have is a recipe for disaster. We either fall off, panic, downclimb, or fail to continue climbing efficiently. Here, anxiety can also influence the feeling of being pumped through epinephrine production (adrenaline).

In an ideal world, we would like to climb a route and only use the right amount of physical and mental energy on each hold/movement. Without wasting energy along the way, that way we can perform to our maximum ability every time.

This section contains a physiological part and a section on the psychology of pumped forearms. Let's start with physiology.

PHYSIOLOGY

When we are climbing, our flexor muscles (forearm) are working to keep ourselves held onto the climbing holds. There is an increased metabolic demand on these muscles, requiring an increase in oxygen and nutrient delivery through increased blood flow to that area. When a muscle contracts, it compresses onto the blood vessels within that muscle and lowers the blood supply to that area.

Hence, as we squeeze our fingers on a hold and tighten the flexor muscles in our forearm, we limit the amount of blood flow to those muscles. When we squeeze 15% of our maximum squeezability (how hard we can grip a hold), we start to occlude blood flow to those muscles. When we squeeze 50% of our maximum squeezability, we stop all blood flow to those muscles. We then rely on the anaerobic lactic energy system, which we have only a limited amount of in our body stores.

When we are scared, we potentially overgrip (grip a hold harder than we need to). We do not want to fall off and end up climbing inefficiently. Using up more energy than we need, allowing less blood flow to those muscles, results in slower recovery. We need oxygenated blood to create energy in our muscles and to flush away the waste product. The harder we squeeze, the sooner we will feel we are getting pumped forearms.

PSYCHOLOGICAL

Here is an article by Brian Rigby written for Climbing magazine, he is a certified sports nutritionist. Brian has worked with many climbers and other athletes. He currently writes a blog (climbingnutrition.com) with science-based information to help climbers perform better and prevent the spread of misinformation and pseudoscience. Here is his view on pumped forearms.

ARTICLE

Learn This: The Over-Gripping Myth

As you move ever higher above your last piece and further outside your comfort zone, you grip the rock for dear life, even though you know the route is well within your ability. Yet here you are, only halfway up and too pumped to continue – everything feels way harder than it should. Most climbers have experienced this unfortunate situation: when you get scared, you hold on too tight and waste precious energy. The perceived solution: focus on relaxing your hands to stop over-gripping the rock, thus lasting longer. While this does seem to make logical sense, over-gripping is actually not a significant factor in this perceived fatigue. Studies in applied physiology, neuroscience, and sports medicine point to stress itself as the culprit for accelerated fatigue. Anxiety can trigger the release of a certain hormone that can make you feel more pumped and tired than you actually are. Here we've provided some tips and tricks to conquer your fears and prevent the dreaded pump.

Physiology of Anxiety

When we attribute poor performance to over-gripping, the situation is usually the same: we're uncomfortable and experiencing a stress response. When we get stressed, whether out of fear, competition, anxiety, or any other worry-inducing factor, we experience a few common physiological changes. Our heart rate increases along with breathing. We switch energy systems from the slow-burning aerobic system, which runs primarily off stored fat, to the faster anaerobic system, which runs primarily off carbohydrates. Our core body temperature starts to rise, and we start to sweat more (another con in climbing). All these changes are mediated through one primary hormone: epinephrine (also called adrenaline), which is necessary when intensity suddenly increases, like powering through a crux.

If the only type of stress we experienced was the stress of exertion on the wall, and the only time we experienced it was during strenuous moves, then epinephrine would only ever be positive. The problem is that fear and anxiety cause stress before we even leave the ground, and therefore cause changes that are less positive/adaptive and more damaging to our performance. A study published in the Journal of Exercise Physiology in 2000 corroborates this: Novice climbers had significantly higher heart rates not only during a climb, but before it even began. The most likely reason for this is anxiety. An increase in mental stress causes an increase in epinephrine release, which then increases heart rate. The novice climbers began the climb with a body already in stress mode – the same physiological state more advanced climbers might only experience during a crux. This means that instead of moving smoothly through the easy sections and reserving stamina for the tough ones, precious energy gets wasted due to an unnecessary increase in epinephrine, caused solely by anxiety.

Damir Spanic

Feel the Pump

The premature release of epinephrine affects performance because the shift to relying on carbohydrates for fuel causes an increase in blood lactate and free hydrogen ions which cause muscular acidosis and the resulting pain. In other words, this increase in intramuscular acid levels causes the burning feeling in your forearms that is associated with pumping out. This increase in pain dampers your endurance and can reduce your resolve to continue, making you feel very pumped and fatigued when in reality, you likely aren't. A 2007 study in the European Journal of Applied Physiology revealed that elite climbers derived 8.5% of their energy from carbohydrates on easy routes. As routes grew in difficulty, this number peaked at roughly 14%. On the other hand, for less-experienced climbers on easy routes, carbohydrate reliance began at 16.5%, almost double the rate for elite climbers.

Perceived Exertion

Anxiety can also explain why we think we are gripping harder, or working harder in general, even if the actual amount of work is not greater. Beyond the physiological changes epinephrine causes, anxiety correlates to perceived exertion, meaning the more anxious you are, the harder everything feels. Perceived exertion isn't just a mental construct; it's how our brain and body communicate during exercise to determine how fatigued we are. Anxiety throws a wrench in the works by increasing perceived exertion, essentially sending the body the wrong signal about how much work is being done and subjecting us to premature fatigue. A second factor that ups perceived exertion is core temperature, which is increased by epinephrine. Actual strength is unaffected, but this increase signals the body to slow down and allow core temperature to decrease. Anxiety, not over-gripping, is the real performance killer here. If we focus primarily on fixing our anxiety, then we fix all the negative elements associated with it. We shift our metabolism back toward burning fat, we cool down our core temperature, and we experience the climb on par with the actual difficulty and our abilities.

Fight Anxiety

Figure out what your source of anxiety is, because you can't change what you don't understand. Are you nervous because you're afraid to take a fall, because you know people are watching, or because the climb is above your usual grade? Once you know the source of your anxiety, create focused strategies (practice falling on the route, visit the crag when it's less busy, etc.).
Give yourself permission to fail. Onsighting problems is great, but the more pressure you put on yourself to perform, the greater your anxiety response will be. When you give yourself permission to fail, you remove your self-imposed consequences, and you'll actually be more likely to succeed.
Learn the climb by heart. In addition to saving energy by increasing your climbing efficiency, you also remove the stress that goes along with new situations. The better you know a route, the less you'll worry about what you might encounter, how far the runout is between bolts, and where you might fall. According to one 2007 applied physiology study, simply repeating a route once decreased anxiety by 16%. Repeating it numerous times will only reduce anxiety further.
Create a pre-climb or pre-comp ritual. We might laugh at the superstitious behaviours of many pro athletes (and their fans) before a game, but these

behaviours have an adaptive advantage — they reduce anxiety. Rituals also help you define meaningful "beginnings" for actions (as in, "After I chalk up three times and clap twice, I begin to climb."), which can help trigger your full concentration on the upcoming task of actually climbing.
Remember that stress is an adaptive response. The reason we experience physiological changes when we're anxious is because they are intended to increase strength, power, focus, and drive, giving us the energy we need to succeed. If you're anxious before a climb, focus on how these positive aspects of the stress response will help you climb, not how the debilitating aspects will hold you back, which can reduce your anxiety about, well, anxiety.

Article taken from Climbing.com (https://www.climbing.com/skills/learn-this-the-over-gripping-myth/)

From the article, we can derive that higher levels of anxiety produce adrenaline (epinephrine), which shifts the body's energy reliance to carbohydrates, resulting in higher levels of lactate, which is one of several causes of muscle fatigue.

Link this with the perception of exertion under stress, and we may feel more tired and pumped than we are.

A simple example of the above would be, if you have ever been on a route, feeling scared and pumped, unable to think clearly about your next move, you eye up the next hold, but think you'll never make it (Chapter 6 – The Influence of Thought), but try anyway.

As a last-ditch effort, you lunge for the next hold, and to your surprise somehow stay on.

CONCLUSION

As climbers, we want to use just the right amount of energy on each hold/ move and be as efficient as possible. Fear can have a detrimental effect on our physiological exertion and psychological perception of our exertion. It is essential to do everything we can to relax to lower our perception of exertion to actual exertion.

Melissa McDonald on Gravedigger (5.12B), Colorado
Bry Manning

Happy Tree Friends, Antalya, Turkey
Moritz Latzka

"THE MIND WITHOUT BORDERS CAN FLY ANYWHERE."

NASIM ESHQI

Will Clarke on 'Solstice' (HVS, 5a), Bus Stop Quarry
Luca Celano

CHAPTER 8

Breathing

"When the breath is unsteady, all is unsteady; when the breath is still; all is still. Control the breath carefully. Inhalation gives strength and a controlled body; retention gives steadiness of mind and longevity; exhalation purifies body and spirit."

SHUKLA SWAMI KUVALAYANANDA

In 1996, whilst scientists worldwide were excited with the birth of Dolly the Sheep, Andrea di Bari discovered the limitless opportunity for the vertical challenges that Kalymnos offered. Endless limestone cliffs, scattered with tufas and pockets, as if purposely carved by history for one purpose only, climbing.

A few decades later, Mateo, a Spanish student from Madrid, made his first pilgrimage to the climbing mecca, Kalymnos. He had his eyes on a route called 'Daniboy', an 8a techy climb, with some dynamic moves. Building up the courage, he finally decided to have a go. After the techy start, he managed to squirm his way into the kneebar under the roof.

Trying to relax as best he can to allow some blood flow back to his arms, he decides its time. Feeling good so far, he works his way from tufa to pocket to tufa – a combination of fear and excitement courses through his veins. The hard work required increases with every inch of height gained.

Fighting pumped forearms and polished holds, unable to think clearly, trying with all his might to stay on, he falls off.

Hanging on the rope, suspended in mid-air above the Spartacus cave, he feels dizzy. "Why am I dizzy?" Mateo thinks to himself. He'd been holding his breath for the last three moves.

Have you ever been on a route, climbed past a section, only to realise you've been holding your breath? This can happen when you feel you are trying hard or when you are scared. But how does holding your breath help when physically exerting yourself?

Why, in a book on the fear of falling, is there a topic on "breathing"? Apart from providing a vital function to stay alive, the way we breathe can positively or negatively affect how we deal with stress. Really?!? Something as simple as breathing.

Brett Jordan

IMPORTANCE OF BREATHING

Without breathing, we would not make it very far. So, from a physiological point of view, we need oxygen in our bodies to stay alive.

Breathing provides oxygen for metabolism and removes carbon dioxide, a waste product. Our body's cells need oxygen to be able to create energy efficiently.

When these cells create energy, they make carbon dioxide. We get oxygen by breathing in and expel carbon dioxide by breathing out.

We can assume that the more we breathe, the more efficient our bodies become to create energy, and the more we get rid of the waste product (carbon dioxide). The more oxygen we take into our bodies, the more energy is created, and the more waste product is expelled. The more energy we have, the longer we can hold on or climb.

Let's talk about the different types of breathing. Really, different types of breathing?!? Isn't it just in and out?!? Let's take a look.

Chest breathing

Chest breathing refers to the type of breathing where we take air into our lungs higher up where the diaphragm is less engaged in the process; this results in shorter, more frequent breaths taking in less oxygen and is usually associated with stress. Nowadays, a high percentage of people chest breathe in their daily lives.

HOW TO?

For this exercise, comfortably sit on a chair, or lie on the floor with knees bent.

1. Close your eyes, place one hand on your chest, and one on your belly.
2. Breathe in through your nose, concentrating on only your chest rising. The hand on your belly should stay still.
3. Then breathe out through your mouth.
4. Do this for 30 seconds. Analyse how you feel.

Belly breathing

Belly breathing, also called abdominal breathing or diaphragmatic breathing is a deep breathing technique that engages your diaphragm. Though the diaphragm is involved in both types of breathing, it is less engaged when chest breathing. The diaphragm is a muscle at the bottom of the ribcage, used in respiration (breathing).

By belly breathing, the body is taking in a greater capacity of air on every breath and can also take less energy to function.

HOW TO?

For this exercise, comfortably sit on a chair, or lie on the floor with knees bent.

1. Close your eyes, place one hand on your chest, and one on your belly.
2. Breathe in through your nose, concentrating on your belly rising. The hand on your chest should stay still.
3. Then breathe out through your mouth.
4. Do this for 30 seconds. Analyse how you feel.

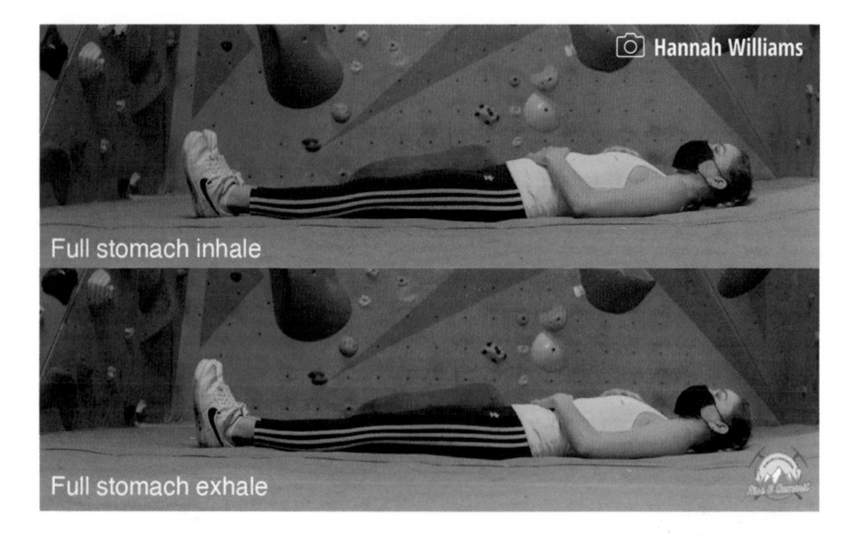

Deep breathing

Deep breathing is associated with abdominal breathing or belly breathing. Here, when belly breathing, your chest will naturally rise as well – allow it to do so. You will feel a greater volume of air travelling through.

With slow deep diaphragm breathing (belly breathing), a greater volume of oxygen is taken in by the lungs, increasing the amount of deoxygenated blood flow back to the lungs and an increase in the amount of oxygenated blood back into the body.

HOW TO?

For this exercise, comfortably sit on a chair, or lie on the floor with knees bent.

1. Close your eyes, place one hand on your chest, and one on your belly.
2. Breathe in through your nose, concentrating on your belly rising first, then allowing the chest to rise.
3. Then breathe out through your mouth.
4. Do this for 30 seconds. Analyse how you feel.

Mouth breathing

Mouth breathing, is as it states, breathing in and out through your mouth. The advantages of breathing air through your mouth are that a larger air capacity can be taken in, and less carbon dioxide is retained.

Both help with metabolism and the creation of energy.

A Japanese study in 2013 found that mouth breathing delivered a disturbance of oxygen to the prefrontal cortex. It was associated with sleep disorders, symptoms of Attention Deficit Hyperactivity Disorder (ADHD), more dental cavities, and an increased flow of oxygen to the prefrontal cortex. What does this mean?

A more active prefrontal cortex means we experience an increase in our cognitive functions, i.e. thinking more. As we know, to be climbing in a state of 'flow', we need to be in a state of transient hypofrontality, where subconscious processing is key. With a more active prefrontal cortex, this is less likely to happen.

Nasal breathing

Breathing through the nose is the way our bodies are designed. The nose is crucial as it filters and heats the air going in, which causes the upper airways to widen, and moistens the air for easier absorption by the lungs. Nasal breathing can lower blood

Hannah Williams

pressure, regulate our heart rate, and apparently help with erectile dysfunction. But not sure this is a topic we should discuss in a climbing book.

In the early 1900's George Catlin, bored with his job as a lawyer, decided to travel the Great Plains in search of Native American tribes. He travelled to over 50 tribes. All of them had one thing in common; they all breathed in and out through their noses. They would close the babies' lips shut after feeding and at night. Cruel right?!? They experienced less sickness and better health.

The sinuses are responsible for releasing nitric oxide when air passes through them and play an essential role in increasing our cells' oxygen uptake. By nasal breathing alone, you can increase oxygen absorption by 18%. So, more oxygen in our bodies means more energy production.

Exhaling

Exhaling refers to the action of breath out of our lungs. An essential part of the breathing process as it expels carbon dioxide from our bodies. Exhaling is neurologically tied to the relaxation process response in the brain.

Hence the idiom – a sigh of relief.

HOW TO?

For this exercise, comfortably sit on a chair, or lie on the floor with knees bent.

1. Close your eyes. Breathe in through your nose, concentrating on your belly rising then your chest.
2. Then breathe out through your mouth, and expel as much air as you can.
3. Then breathe in again through your nose, concentrating on your belly and chest rising (make sure you have a steady pace of breathing, i.e. 5–6 seconds in, 5–6 seconds out).
4. Do this for 30 seconds. Analyse how you feel.

Most of us only use 10% of the diaphragm, which overburdens the heart and raises blood pressure. As we inhale, we decrease the intrathoracic pressure moving down the diaphragm, increasing abdominal pressure, thus allowing more oxygen-depleted blood to travel to the lungs. By exhaling, the opposite happens, encouraging oxygen-rich blood to flow through our bodies. So, the greater the exhalation, the more oxygen-rich blood flowing through our bodies.

Slow and rhythmic breathing

At our usual breathing rate, our lungs absorb a quarter of the oxygen in the air. The rest we exhale out. When we slow our breathing rate down, we allow our lungs to soak up more oxygen in fewer breaths.

Patricia Gerbarg and Richard Brown experimented with slow breathing patterns on their patients who suffered from anxiety and depression. They found that inhaling for 5.5 seconds and exhaling for 5.5 seconds synchronises with our cardiovascular (Siegmund Mayer) rhythms.

Dr Alan Watkins also stipulates the importance of rhythmic breathing. Where breath in is a certain length, and breath out is a certain length (i.e. 4 seconds in, 6 seconds out, or 5 seconds in, 5 seconds out). When there is rhythm in our breathing rate, this will cause our hearts to have a consistent rate. As the heart is the brain's power station, an erratic heart rate will impair our brain function, which happens in a fight-or-flight response. With a steady breathing rate and a balanced heart rate, our brain will be in a state of coherence. Dr Watkins also stipulates the importance of a smooth, steady breath in and a steady breath out, meaning an even and constant rate.

EFFECTS OF BREATHING

Breathing is the motherboard to the autonomic nervous system, which has two parts; the sympathetic and the parasympathetic nervous system. The sympathetic nervous system is responsible for increasing arousal in a fearful situation. The parasympathetic nervous system is in charge of the rest response.

Breathing is an essential aspect of the brain's function and dealing with stress, anxiety, and fear. In a moment of fear/anxiety, rapid breathing will ready the body for fight-or-flight, bringing your senses to a heightened state of readiness and activating the amygdala – responsible for fear activity within the brain.

With slow deep breaths, we take fewer breaths, and a greater volume of air enters the lungs, using more of the lungs' space – instead of shallower breaths of a higher frequency with lower intake. A study has proven that slow deep breathing is more efficient than shallow and faster breathing at supplying oxygen to our bloodstream, which our metabolic system needs to create energy.

Slow and deep breathing results in a relative increase in activity in the parasympathetic nervous system (PSNS), which is responsible for rest. When activated, it encourages energy conservation, slows the heart rate, and relaxes your muscles.

The lungs are covered with nerve endings connected to both the sympathetic and parasympathetic nervous systems. Many of the nerve endings in the lower part of the lungs are connected to the PSNS. Hence, long deep and slow breaths are relaxing. Upon a deep breath in, exhaling stimulates an even stronger parasympathetic response.

So, how is this relevant to the fear of falling? When we become fearful in a moment of stress, slow and deep breathing slows down the heart rate and relaxes us, the opposite of fear; this is where breathing is even more so important. Deep slow breathing also results in endorphins being produced in the body (which is a chemical in the body that relieves us from stress and pain).

Studies have shown that controlled breathing can lower the levels of cortisol (stress hormone) present in the saliva and alter brain chemistry, which helps enhance focus.

How to breathe well?

1. Have a steady rhythm
2. Smoothness in and out
3. Matching the length of inhalation and exhalation
4. Using both the abdomen and chest to breathe
5. Breathe in through the nose and out through the mouth

Next time you go climbing, try some of the following exercises:

EXERCISE 8.1

Climb a familiar route of medium difficulty as you usually would. Come back down, have a rest. Once rested, try it again. Before you set off, take 3-4 slow deep and rhythmic breaths, using both abdomen and chest to breathe in through your nose and out through your mouth; now climb.
Analyse if you feel a difference in perceived effort.

EXERCISE 8.2

As above, climb a familiar route of medium difficulty as you normally would. Come back down, have a rest. Once rested, try it again. Now try and breathe on every move you make. In through your nose, out through your mouth, remembering to keep a steady rhythm. When breathing out, force most of the air out of your lungs, forcing you to take more air in (*). It can be helpful to do this out loud. You may become very self-conscious trying out this exercise but stick with it. Analyse if you feel a difference in perceived effort.
(*) Note: you can also try and time the exhale with an increase in effort (i.e. every time you pull up on a hold/move). As the yogis do, "Inhale, prepare, exhale on effort.".

EXERCISE 8.3

Here you can use both breathing techniques from exercise 1 & 2 on a familiar route and notice if you experience any difference in perceived effort. Once you get the hang of these, try using them on a route where you may experience a small amount of stress. Analyse how you feel afterwards.

Again, the importance here is practice. The more you practice, the more these become habits and part of your routine.

Practice on easier terrain, and slowly introduce these techniques on more challenging terrain. The more you practice these, the better you'll get at them.

Just remember, your brain is neuroplastic (malleable), even in old age.

CONCLUSION

Most of us underestimate the importance of breathing, and it is something we take for granted. Slow, deep, rhythmic nasal-breathing into your belly is beneficial to us by having greater energy levels, feeling calmer, and being more energy-efficient. When in a moment of stress, focus on breathing through your nose, deep and slow, with a steady rhythm into your belly. You will feel more relaxed and less stressed as long as the stress you are exposed to is manageable and matches your skill level.

Wogü (8c), Rätikon, Switzerland

Marc Daviet

“

TO ME, CLIMBING IS NOT ABOUT CRIMPING SMALL HOLDS, IT’S A WAY TO MOVE ON THE ROCK, LIKE A DANCE. IT’S AN INVITATION TO FEEL ONE WITH NATURE AND TO EXPRESS OURSELVES AS ARTISTS.

”

NINA CAPREZ

Climbing wall in Copenhagen, Denmark
Victor Xok

CHAPTER 9

The Belayer-Climber Relationship

"The rope connecting two men on a mountain is more than nylon protection; it is an organic thing that transmits subtle messages of intent and disposition from man to man; it is an extension of the tactile senses, a psychological bond, a wire along which currents of communication flow."

TREVANIAN (FROM THE EIGER SANCTION)

The climber and belayer relationship can be an unspoken close bond, hopefully, full of banter, sarcasm, mickey-taking, emotional support, and friendship. It is a significant relationship built on trust. When that unspoken trust exists, it allows the climber to immerse him/herself in the act of climbing entirely. The belayer holds the climber's fate in their hands.

This responsibility is not always taken very seriously; I far too often see (mainly indoors) the belayer using a climbing centre as a social hub. It is, but sometimes being indoors between 4 walls gives people that false sense of security. Whilst the climber is battling on the crux, the belayer is talking to someone else or looking at eye candy (mainly talking about the boys here), increasing the probability of an accident. This is unacceptable, even on the easier routes.

I have fallen off plenty of climbs, which I would consider well within my ability. Especially in an indoor setting, the belayer can sometimes forget that they are holding someone's life in their hands. So, treat it like that. Pay attention at all times, no excuses.

The perfect relationship between climber and belayer would be the climber concentrating on climbing and clipping (or placing protection) and the belayer doing everything else. The relationship can develop to the point where no communication is required because the belayer can anticipate the climber's every movement and knows what to do and when – working in perfect harmony.

Below are some suggestions for both the belayer and climber and their roles.

THE PERFECT BELAYER

What could the belayer do to instil confidence in the climber?

1. Encouragement – Some climbers like encouragement shouted to them whilst on a route; others prefer to be in their own little world. But as a belayer, find out what your partner prefers and find out what helps them.
2. Buddy checks – I have been climbing for a very long time, and still to this day, I check my partners' knot or check their belay device and carabiner have been tied in properly, sometimes seeing if the harness has been tied on properly and vice versa. This is in no way a judgement on someone's personal ability, and the ego should be moved aside for this. For me, when I'm about to climb a project, I get butterflies and get a little nervous/excited, and it gives me the reassurance when my belay partner checks my knot for me – ensuring that everything has been tied well – One less thing to worry about.
3. Keeping rope taut for the first 5–6m (or the first three clips), then slowly ease off – I guess this is obvious, but see too many people giving out too much slack low down. If we are talking about an indoor sport route, there is the potential for a ground fall, even by the 4–5th clip. So, keep the rope taut (I know, this will be a harder catch, but at least the climber will not hit the floor), and gently ease off as the climber gets higher (taut means not tight, as the climber will need some freedom of movement, and a tight rope may affect their climbing).

4. Dynamic belaying – This is where the belayer slightly lengthens the climber's fall to soften the impact. The belayer moves with the rope as the climber hits the end of the rope, reducing the force on the climber, hence a softer catch (this can only be done after a certain height, please use careful judgement, if unsure, please ask an instructor for some guidance).*

5. Active belaying – This is where you as the belayer – instead of taking in rope and giving out slack on every small movement the climber makes – you walk towards the wall and away from the wall to reduce or give a little slack; this can be a very efficient way of belaying. Can only be used on a surface where there is no probability of falling, i.e. usually outside on uneven terrain, it may not be safe to do so.*

6. Judging the potential falling arc – By this, I mean that as the belayer, it is your responsibility to give out more or less slack on the rope so that if the climber were to fall, they would miss any of the obstacles in his/her way. For example, ledges, stepped overhangs, volumes, or any other obstacle they may hit on the way down.
7. Judging the movement of the climber – As the belayer, when you have built up a bit of experience and a relationship with the climber, you will be able to judge most if not all of their movements. You will be able to see when they will move up when they are going to pull the rope up to clip, and when they may be stressed and more likely to fall off. The last thing the climber wants is when they are on the crux move and need slack, and the rope is pulling them down. Here, frustration and tension can build very quickly.
8. Focus only on the climber – As the belayer, your eyes must be upon the climber at all times so that you can judge what is happening/going to happen. If you have not bought a pair of belay glasses yet, I suggest you do. A little strange to use at first, but these save your neck and allow you to watch the climber at all times comfortably. They also help prevent distractions. There is nothing worse than trying to pull up some slack, ready to clip, on the crux move on a route, and your belayer is not giving out rope because his/her attention is elsewhere.
9. Communicate mistakes – By this, I mean when the climber has his/her leg under the rope, back clipped a quickdraw, doing a lot of very high clipping, possibly Z-clipping, etc., tell the climber. Sometimes the climber may be stressed on a route, and they are just focusing on climbing and may make a small mistake; it's your responsibility as the belayer to communicate that.

* *Refer to end of this chapter on how to access video linked with QR code.*

THE PERFECT CLIMBER

What can the climber do?

1. Buddy checks – As mentioned before, I have been climbing for a very long time. To this day, I check my partners' knots, check their belay device and carabiner have been tied in properly, sometimes seeing if the harness has been tied on correctly, and vice versa. So, before I'm about to set off on a climb, I will check the belayer has put the rope through the belay device as it should be and locked the carabiner attached to it.
2. Safety first – Whether climbing indoors or outdoors, if I'm on a sport route, where I may fall off low down, and have the ability to clip the first 1 or 2 clips (using a clip stick outside; climbing easier routes indoors, clipping the second clip, then come down), I will. I understand that some climbers out there will be very judgemental about this and will be adamant that this is not the 'proper' way or 'clean' climbing. Well, who cares? I love climbing, and I love being injury-free. I will clip the first bolt of most outdoor sport routes and do this on indoor routes where I may fall off before the 1st or 2nd clip. In an indoor setting, you usually have good route setters that will keep this in mind, but better to be safe than sorry. As an example, a twisted ankle can take 6–8 weeks to heal. That would mean 6–8 weeks of no climbing; that is a long time when you are in it.

Lary Arce on Inflación 8a,
Hatún Machay, Perú
Diego López

3. Clip the quickdraws between shoulder and hips – What some of us like to do, is clip a quickdraw when we can reach it; this is sometimes around or above head height. If we are scared, we tend to high-clip as it gives us a sense of security, but we increase the potential fall distance. When we are closer to the ground, we increase the probability of a ground fall. Scan the following QR code, which will show the consequences of bad belaying and high clipping.*
4. Falling properly – When as climbers we fall off, it is important that we slightly push off the wall, especially when the terrain we are climbing is a slab or vertical, so as to not cheese grate on the wall on the way down. It is also very important to fall properly (please see Chapter 11 – Falling Exercises).
5. Climb safely – As a climber, be aware of where you are on the wall, i.e. clipping in safe positions, not straying far from the climbing line – so that you will not have a big swing when you do fall – to have no limbs tangled around the rope, and communicate to your belayer if necessary.
6. Positive affirmation – When you feel the belayer has done a good job, i.e. communication, soft catches, encouragement whilst you were climbing the crux, etc., mention this to him/her. It is always nice to know, as a belayer, you have done a good job. But also communicate if there is room for improvement. We all want to get better at what we do.

It is very important to have this unspoken bond between climber and belayer. By building up all of these good habits as climbers and belayers, you take away those tiny details that may affect your climbing performance. So, all you need to concentrate on as a climber is the climbing itself and dealing with your own mind. The relationship is built on trust. If, on the other hand, you have a belayer who decides not to pay attention or change for the better and you feel it affects your climbing, you may need to take hard action and break up with them.

*Use your mobile phone in the camera function to scan the QR code. This will take you to a link with a video. The video is password-protected and case sensitive, password is:

Psychology

If you have any problems accessing the QR codes, please email me on info@riseandsummit.co.uk

Semi-finals in Briançon 2019

Eddie Fowke

“

TRAINING SHOULD BE FUN, HARD, CHALLENGING, BUT MOST OF ALL A SYSTEMATIC APPROACH TO BECOMING A BETTER ATHLETE. ENJOY THE PROCESS!

”

SEAN MCCOLL

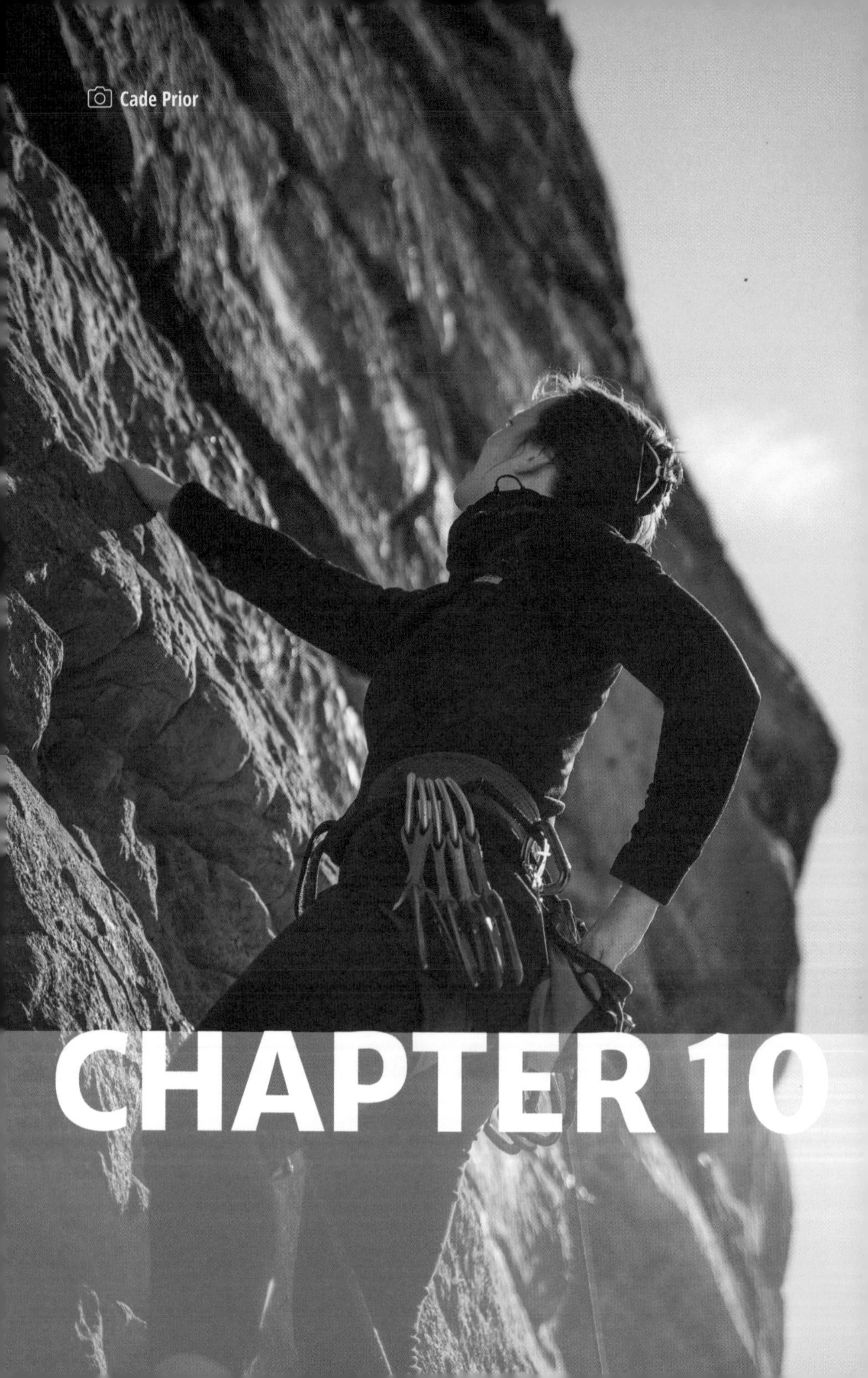

Cade Prior

CHAPTER 10

Coping Strategies

"It goes, boys!"

LYNN HILL
AFTER THE FIRST FREE ASCENT OF THE NOSE

There I was, on El Cap all alone, with no-one to help me. I was on a section of slab with no edges or handholds to pull or crank on. "How I hate slab climbing." I thought to myself.

I was above my last piece of gear, and the realisation of loneliness and fear became overwhelming. There was no one to shout abuse at me, words of encouragement, or sarcasm to take my mind off the ever-increasing sensation of fear. I could feel my heart beating in my throat and the pores on my tired and worn hands lubricating my fingertips. "My body is just not helping." I thought.

In a moment of enlightenment, I remembered that it might help to focus on my breathing. I took a few deep breaths and felt the fight-or-flight response subside a little. I needed to focus on climbing to the next piece of gear, which would lead to easier climbing. A little voice in my head reminded me to focus on the small intricacies and the texture of the rock. Looking at all of its imperfections that stood the test of time, from its creation through the process of being shaped by glaciers. As if someone had chiselled the perfect protrusion to get some friction. I became so hyper-focused on that small crystal; it became the size of an ample handhold in my mind. Fear seemed to have dissipated, as I now had a different focus.

In a moment of fear, it is very easy to forget how to manage our feelings. Here we have a comprehensive list of strategies; some are to be used in a moment of fear, when on a route, or knowing that you may experience fear as you are trying a project, or just pushing your comfort zone. Others can be incorporated as part of the greater picture. Some of these may work; some of these may not. It is up to you to play around with them and see how they work for you. Some of these strategies may work for you but will need consistent practice and patience for new neural pathways to set in your brain.

Sam Simpson on 'The Ticks ate all the Midges' (7a+), Moy Rock
Luca Celano

COPING STRATEGIES – DEALING WITH FEAR IN CLIMBING

BREATHING

Breathing (Chapter 8 – Breathing) is an essential aspect of the brain's function when dealing with stress, anxiety, and fear. In a moment of fear/anxiety, rapid breathing will ready the body for fight or flight, bringing your senses to a heightened state of readiness and activating the amygdala responsible for fear activity within the brain.

Slow and deep breathing results in a relative increase in activity of the parasympathetic nervous system (PSNS). The PSNS is responsible for rest. When activated, it encourages energy conservation, slows down the heart rate, and relaxes your muscles.

So, take deep, slow breaths in through the nose and out through the mouth in moments of stress. Focus on the feeling of the breath (i.e. the raising and lowering of the belly and chest, the way the air enters the lungs and as it pushes out, etc.).

This can be done before or during climbing a route where you think you may fall off. Something I do is breathe on every move I make; that way, I lower my stress levels and supply my body with as much oxygen as possible, so my body can produce energy where it is needed. Concentrating on breathing will focus your mind on something other than what's coming up; that way, you are in the moment.

FOCUS

You can combine the above (breathing) with a very concentrated focus on different elements. The feeling of your fingertips on the hold, its texture, a small pebble sticking out of the rock, your toes on the holds. I am talking about an intense focus, where what you decide to focus on becomes the only thing you can see/feel. Focus on the texture of the hold, the tiny granules you can see on a rock. Look at the tiny lines on your fingers. Or think about how a hold feels, visualise it, and focus on this. You can even close your eyes to help with this.

Once you feel that fear has lessened a little, take a few deep breaths, and move on, even if it is one more move, it is all progress.

RELAX

If you combine slow and deep breathing with focusing on relaxing your muscles throughout the body. It may help to close your eyes, as long as it is safe to do so, and focus on the tension held in your body. Focus on trying to relax those muscles as much as possible. Then take a few more breaths before trying to move on, even if it is one more move. The benefit of this is that by relaxing specific muscles, you allow more blood flow to those areas; hence, the body can regenerate, and you feel your energy being restored. Continue when you feel relaxed, even if it is one more move. It is all progress.

"The more relaxed the muscles are, the more energy can flow through the body. Using muscular tension to try 'do' the punch or attempting the brute force to knock someone over will only work to opposite effect."
BRUCE LEE

DELAY

As mentioned in chapter 2 (Scripts and Behavioural Patterns), even by delaying your usual sequences of scripts (habits), you are putting in small changes to the neural pathway you would usually follow. In a moment of fear, hang on the same holds, and delay your usual sequence of events. Stay there for 1 second before going back down or shouting take. Next time, delay by 2 seconds and so on. Just by delaying the habit, you are instilling small changes. Be patient with yourself.

Climber competing in the Winter Comp at the Warehouse Climbing Centre
Mike Chrimes

FREQUENT PRACTICE

Well, that goes without saying. To become good or accustomed to something, we need to practice it. Frequent falling practice, starting within your comfort zone, then slowly building this up. If you practice falling at the start of each climbing session, you will get rid of the butterflies (or most of them) and climb better as a result for the rest of your session. The more you practice, the more your body and mind will modify its comfort zone (VERY IMPORTANT). Every climbing session I have on ropes, I will have to fall off at some point, to keep consistency, and to keep my comfort zone at that level or to grow it.

VISUALISATION

Before climbing a route, visualise every move (hands and feet), clipping, what you may feel, feeling on the crux, falling off (and the consequences of falling off), when you get to the top and remind yourself of your motivation to attempt your project. This mental rehearsal almost equates to having climbed the route and can help reduce mental noise during climbing (see more on visualisation in Chapter 13 – Performance Anxiety).

POSITIVE AFFIRMATION

Negative thoughts will pass through your mind; you are not these thoughts; these happen because of uncertainty (something that has not happened yet – self-doubt – or an experience). Observe these negative thoughts, and affirm yourself with positive talk, i.e. "I can do it", "I am safe", etc. As we looked at in chapter 6 – The Influence of Thought , be kind to yourself and describe yourself using positive affirmation only.

PERFORMANCE PRESSURE AND EXPECTATIONS

Alleviate the pressure of performing. The pressure you put upon yourself to perform can cause you to climb in a physiologically and psychologically tense state. As a Chinese philosopher once said,

"When archers shoot for enjoyment, they have all their skill;
when they shoot for a brass buckle, they get nervous;
when they shoot for a prize of gold, they begin to see two targets.".

Sometimes the harder you try, the tenser you may feel, and the more your performance can be affected. On the days when I do not feel like climbing or find I'm not motivated, I tend to climb better, as I have no expectations of my performance.

THE LEARNING PROCESS

In our way of life, we are conditioned to focus on the outcome. From the moment we go to school and throughout our work life. With this comes a lot of pressure to achieve. Instead, focus on the learning process and the next small step required to get closer to achieving your goal. Use positive affirmation to acknowledge your achievements, however small these may be. Some days you may not feel like progress has happened. These days happen, it's all ok. Think about where you started and where you are now.

PLANNING

Write a plan about what goals you would like to achieve, possibly on a monthly calendar chart. Write down the individual steps you will need to take to achieve these goals. Try to work with this, but remember this can be dynamic, and adjust accordingly. If you have this chart to hand, you can see how your progress over time and use it as motivation to keep track of your development.

Just remember that each of these steps should comprise of achievable goals within the process. Even if you have to repeat some of the techniques, progress will happen; just be patient.

You can also write down anything positive that may have happened every time you go climbing, however small this may be. And look back at this after a few months, you can then see the progress that has happened, an incentive to keep going.

Andrew Finney on 'Heading the Shot' (7a+), Seamstress Slab, Serengeti
Luca Celano

STOP, COMPOSE YOURSELF, AND CONTINUE

In a moment of stress, or when you can feel stress building or doubt creeping in, STOP. Stop climbing; accept how you are feeling. Pause for long enough to regroup your thoughts, focus on a broader view (i.e. look around), then continue climbing. Look to the left or right (broader view, not tunnel vision), where you focus on the broader picture or look through the view (a bit like the optical illusion pictures which you have to focus beyond the image to see the illusion). Where you are not focused on any one element in your vision, but almost looking through it, where nothing is really in focus. It may seem a little like day dreaming. You can combine this strategy with breathing.

CREATE MORE TENSION

Creating more tension when you are anxious or stressed, sounds counter-intuitive. You can try this before you are about to climb or in a moment of fear whilst on a climb. Breathe in, tense all your muscles, as well as your lungs holding your breath, then on the breath out, focus on relaxing all of your muscles. Follow this with deep belly breathing – this will cause you to feel more relaxed than you were in your state of fear or anxiety.

Now continue climbing, even if it is one more move.

SELF-HYPNOSIS

Self-hypnosis is a state of heightened awareness and relaxation that is self-induced. Before setting off on a climb (that you think may create stress), concentrate on tension in your body and focus on relaxing this tension. Close your eyes, relax your shoulder muscles, allow your arms to hang beside you. Relax your head, count back from 20, imagine being in a complete state of relaxation using an image that makes you feel relaxed (for more details, see Chapter 13 – Performance Anxiety). Then when you feel comfortable, set off on your climb.

SING A SONG

Sing a song whilst climbing, in your head or out loud. I guess this is a judgement you have to make, whether you have a good voice or a forgiving audience. I know it may sound silly, but some high-performance athletes sing songs to themselves when they realise they are putting themselves in a stressful situation, as it causes you to be more relaxed as you remain focused on the singing. If you like, you can even throw in some head bobbing or hip swings in there. The exercise can be used to distract your mind. You will feel your anxious thoughts diminishing or disappearing. It is just like counting sheep to help fall asleep.

If you struggle to sing a song, listen to some music you like, loud enough so you can hear it on the crux, and mime your way up.

WHISTLE

Whistling whilst in a moment of stress or when climbing when you knowingly are going to put yourself in a moment of stress can be helpful too. Whistling causes small vibrations in some of the facial muscles, physiological structures, and organs, putting the whistler in a pleasurable and relaxed state. Whistling also forces you to breathe at a regular and steady rhythm, using your diaphragm (belly) to breathe; as we saw in Chapters 1 & 8, this kind of breathing kickstarts the PSNS, which in turn relaxes the whistler. The same goes for the vagus nerve (see Chapter 13 – Performance Anxiety). Through regular, steady abdominal breathing (belly), the vagus nerve is stimulated, lowering the heart rate, which calms us down and relaxes our entire body.

As well as refocusing the pre-frontal cortex, which can only think of one thing at a time, allowing the subconscious to climb, it can be relaxing as it is a form of music. But this part depends on how good your whistling is.

BE EXPRESSIVE

Swear, shout, scream or get angry. It is a way of relieving tension and frustration or used to take the edge off anxiety.

If you do decide to swear, please be mindful of your audience.

CLIMB FAST

Climb a route fast and without thinking; this does not give your mind time to overthink and will remain in the present, thinking about the next hold. You can always add deep and slow breathing or breathe on each move.

PRE-PERFORMANCE ROUTINE

Have a specific routine that you run through before each climb. After having done the route reading – tie in, put your shoes on, remember the buddy checks, look at the floor, chalk up your hands, take 2–3 deep breaths, shake hands, then start. Going through this process works for me as it helps me get rid of any unrelated negative thoughts and remain focused on the task at hand (more details on creating your own pre-performance routine in Chapter 13 – Performance Anxiety).

MOST IMPORTANTLY

Have fun whilst climbing. Use as much sarcasm, mickey-taking, and jokes to lighten the mood (if this works for you).

Try not to take yourself and others too seriously. But be aware of each other's sense of humour, as we do not want to end up abusing one another unless that is what you like. A feeling of disappointment of not climbing your project can quickly be diffused by jokes (very British). Take the pressure off performing at times. It is only climbing and meant to be fun.

FINAL WORD

Just remember that being afraid is very typical within climbing. The more you practice and the more experience you have, the easier this becomes to deal with it. When you are afraid (assuming you are not in a deadly situation), one tends to base fear on something that MAY happen – or on a historical experience. So when you are on that crux move above a bolt, and you don't know whether you can make it or not, don't fall into the trap of allowing fear to manifest itself and control you. Make sure progress happens at your pace.

Try all or any of the above methods. Some may work for you; some may not. These are very individual, and what works for you may not work for someone else. But please, remember, practice makes perfect, lots of practice.

Let me know if you have other strategies which have not been mentioned. Please email me at info@riseandsummit.co.uk; I always like to hear others' perspectives.

Salva Mea 8a, Foxhole, Gower

Paul Wood

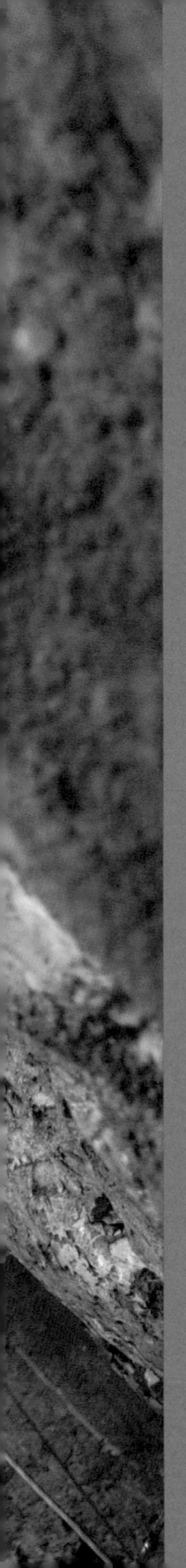

“

FOR ME, CLIMBING AT ONE’S LIMIT IS ALL ABOUT ENJOYMENT. I’VE ALWAYS HAD MOST SUCCESS WHEN THE PROCESS WAS A PLEASURE. PURSUE GOALS THAT INVOLVE DOING WHAT YOU LOVE AND YOU WILL ACHIEVE THEM.

”

CAILEAN HARKER

Long Duong on Chain Reaction (5.12c), Smith Rock
Todd Tang

CHAPTER 11

Falling Exercises

On being asked why, at the age of 93, he still devoted 3 hours a day to practising, Pablo Casals said – ***"I'm beginning to notice some improvement."***

ONE OF THE GREATEST CELLISTS OF ALL TIME

As climbers, we are really good at training physically to get stronger. But why, when climbing requires a strong mental game, do we forget about mental training?

The following are a list of exercises you can play with when climbing. These are to be used intentionally. It is a list of progressive exercises to be used over time, looking at working in your learning zone, where it is exciting, but you are still in control. Start in the comfort zone, and build it up, slowly. Combine these with the list of the coping strategies and other elements we have looked at in previous chapters.

Again, I need to stress the importance of regular practice. Through repetition and gradual exposure, we can retrain our mind on what we find manageable. Have realistic and achievable goals set within your sessions.

Before we go onto the progressive falling exercises, lets first talk about how to fall.

HOW TO FALL?

When we learn to climb, that is precisely what we do. We learn to climb and fine-tune our techniques. There is, however, a place for learning how to fall. It is essential to prevent injury and build confidence in ourselves, the belayer, and the equipment. We do not want to fall off the wall like a wet pancake sliding out of the pan. When falling off a climb/route, we need to:

1. Be relaxed
2. Slightly push away from the wall (if on vertical or slab terrain)
3. Look between legs as we fall
4. Have arms and legs out and not grab the rope

HOW TO FALL

1. Relaxed

We need to be as relaxed as possible through the action of deep breathing. When we identify falling with being relaxed, we retrain the mind and form new neural pathways and create positive associations. Please see first section of the following video.*

2. Slight push away from the wall

To not cheese grate the wall on the way down; this is especially important if you are climbing vertical walls or slabs. Please see second section of the following video.*

3. Eyes down between feet

As we fall off, we need to direct our eyes between our feet. By doing so, we can see obstacles on the way down, and we also psychologically become accustomed faster to being at height and falling. Instead of closing your eyes or looking up, try looking down. Please see third section of the following video.*

* *Refer to end of this chapter on how to access video linked with QR code.*

4. Arms and legs out, and no rope grabbing

The reason we grab the rope as we fall is mostly psychological reassurance, but if not tied in, you could never hold the rope on a fall. We have our arms and legs out to protect ourselves from possible impact with the wall. The only times you can grab the rope is to stop tipping backwards when falling under an overhang. Sometimes top-heavy climbers will need to grab the rope, to prevent themselves from tipping back.

Another reason for not grabbing the rope is that you may get a finger, thumb, or hand caught around the rope, resulting in a severe injury. Please see fourth section of the following video.*

BELAYING WITH FALLING EXERCISES

When doing any of the falling exercises, it is crucial to learn how to belay dynamically.

By dynamic belaying, you are trying to reduce the impact force directed to the climber. In doing so, you are providing a softer catch. Please follow the QR code, which will explain further how to belay dynamically.*

PROGRESSIVE EXERCISES FOR LEAD CLIMBING

Before we get into the exercises, pick a slightly overhanging route with big holds.

Make sure it feels easy to climb for your level. Lead climb your way up and clip the first six quickdraws. Get the belayer to take in, then lower you to the ground.

With these exercises, there must be a lot of trust between the climber and belayer. Only progress at the pace of the climber. As the belayer, be patient and do not force anything. You can be encouraging, but don't feed out a load of slack on purpose because you think you are helping, as this can have the opposite effect.

* *Refer to end of this chapter on how to access video linked with QR code.*

It can help to use an assisted braking belay device to instil confidence in the climber and provide reassurance with an extra safety element.
These exercises can be mentally draining, so when you feel you have worked through a number of them. Relax, and have some fun climbing. Get back to them in the next session.

We need to have all four falling elements under our belt before attempting the progression in the following exercises. Practice these in a no-stress situation. Incorporate these on all of the below exercises and games. Firstly, practice them on a tight top rope before moving on. By this I mean on a top rope, ask the belayer to take the rope in tight, then let go of the wall. You need to have all four elements of falling well practised on each exercise until they become autonomous before moving on to the next one.*

It is very important to practice these exercises, but only move on when you feel there is no feeling of fear involved.

With the following exercises, it is best to start with exercise one and build it up, even though some of you may already have some falling experience. I know some of you will want to skip a few, but it is worthwhile being patient. (Note: if you are struggling to let go of the holds/wall with some of the exercises, try clapping your hands a few times – pull into the wall/rock, clap, grab the holds again, do this a few times, then let go).

We also need to build confidence in the whole system. If you move too quickly through the exercises, you may find yourself missing out on one of the elements. If this happens, revisit the previous exercise.

Each of the exercises and games is marked with the level of belayer needed for the exercise. As this is a very important part of the process, the belayer needs lots of practice to get better at dynamic belaying and judging the amount of slack that is appropriate in the system. If you are in doubt, please ask a local instructor to observe where they think you may be or give you some pointers.

* *Refer to end of this chapter on how to access video linked with QR code.*

The three categories are:

Beginner Belayer – comfortable with top rope belaying.

Intermediate Belayer – comfortable with lead belaying and has caught some falls on lead climbing.

Advanced belayer – comfortable with lead belaying and catching lead falls. Able to judge distances in slack paid out to prevent a falling climber from hitting obstacles on the way down. Able to provide soft catches through dynamic belaying.

EXERCISE 1

Climb up the route (the first six quickdraws are clipped) to 1–2 metres below the last clipped quickdraw.

Just like a top rope – Get the belayer to take the rope tight and let go of the wall. You are now hanging. Now bounce around on the rope as hard as you can. Don't just do it once; see if you can break any of the equipment. No luck, right. Keep doing it until it feels comfortable, and no feeling of fear/adrenaline is involved.*

EXERCISE 2

Climb up the chosen route to 1–2 metres below the last clipped quickdraw. Get the belayer to take the rope taut (not tight). Do not let the belayer take in any more rope, and just hold on (do not move up). Focus on your breathing, try to be as relaxed as possible, then let go, and push out a little. Making sure you look down as you fall, keep your hands and feet out to protect yourself, and refrain from grabbing the rope. Repeat this process until there is no feeling of fear/adrenaline involved, and you tick all of the "how to fall" criteria (relaxed, push off, look between legs, no rope grabbing, hands and feet out).*

* *Refer to end of this chapter on how to access video linked with QR code.*

EXERCISE 3

Now repeat exercise two.
When you (as the climber) pull back on the wall, make one move and be sure the belayer does not take in any more rope. So, you will be falling on a slightly slack rope. Repeat this process until there is no feeling of fear/adrenaline involved, and you feel ready to move on.*

EXERCISE 4

Now repeat exercise two.
When you (as the climber) pull back on the wall, make two moves and ensure the belayer does not take in any more rope. So, you will be falling on a slightly slacker rope. Repeat this process until there is no feeling of fear/adrenaline involved, and you feel ready to move on.*

EXERCISE 5

Now climb with the last clipped quickdraw at head level. Get the belayer to have a little bit of slack in the system, making sure you tick all of the "how to fall" criteria. Repeat this process until there is no feeling of fear/adrenaline involved, and you feel ready to move on.*

EXERCISE 6

Now repeat exercise 5, make one more move, make sure the belayer does not take any more rope in, and then let go, making sure you tick all of the "how to fall" criteria.

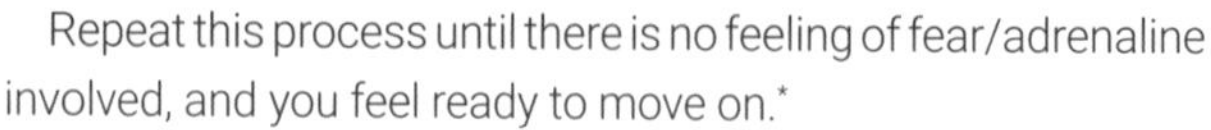

Repeat this process until there is no feeling of fear/adrenaline involved, and you feel ready to move on.*

* *Refer to end of this chapter on how to access video linked with QR code.*

EXERCISE 7

Now repeat exercise 5, make two more moves, make sure the belayer does not take any more rope in, and then let go, making sure you tick all of the "how to fall" criteria.

Repeat this process until there is no feeling of fear/adrenaline involved, and you feel ready to move on.*

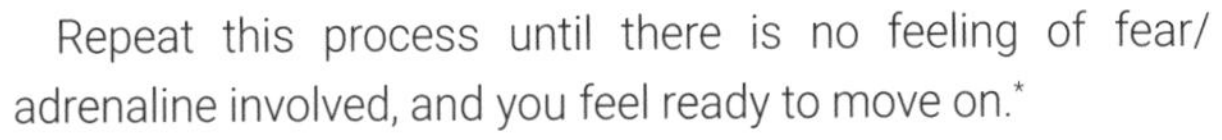

EXERCISE 8

Now climb with the last clipped quickdraw at waist level. Get the belayer to take in with only a little slack available in the system, then let go, making sure you tick all of the "how to fall" criteria. Repeat this process until there is no feeling of fear/adrenaline involved, and you feel ready to move on.*

EXERCISE 9

Now repeat exercise 8, and make one more move, making sure the belayer gives a little more slack here, as you will be moving above the clip, then let go, making sure you tick all of the "how to fall" criteria. Repeat this process until there is no feeling of fear/adrenaline involved, and you feel ready to move on.

EXERCISE 10

Now repeat exercise 8, make two more moves, make sure the belayer gives a little more slack here, as you will be moving above the clip, then let go, making sure you tick all of the "how to fall" criteria. Repeat this process until there is no feeling of fear/adrenaline involved, and you feel ready to move on.

* *Refer to end of this chapter on how to access video linked with QR code.*

For the following exercises, make sure you are a little higher, as the falling distance would be greater. If you need to clip the rope to a higher quickdraw, repeat some of the previous exercises to make sure you have become accustomed to falling at that height.

EXERCISE 11

Now climb with the last clipped quickdraw at foot level, making sure the belayer gives a little more slack here, then let go, making sure you tick all of the "how to fall" criteria. Repeat this process until there is no feeling of fear/adrenaline involved, and you feel ready to move on.*

EXERCISE 12

Now climb with the last clipped quickdraw at foot level, and touch the next quickdraw, making sure the belayer gives a little more slack here, as you will be moving above the clip, then let go, making sure you tick all of the "how to fall" criteria. Repeat this process until there is no feeling of fear/adrenaline involved, and you feel ready to move on.*

EXERCISE 13

Now climb with the last clipped quickdraw at foot level, pull the rope up as if you are going to clip the next quickdraw, but let go before making the next clip. Be sure you tick all of the "how to fall" criteria. Repeat this process until there is no feeling of fear/adrenaline involved, and you feel ready to move on. Please note: Make sure you are high enough to fall off here safely as this is the exercise where there will be the most amount of slack in the system.*

Exercise 13 is the longest distance you should be falling in an indoor setting. With a good belayer, there should not be much difference between the distance fallen on exercise 12 and 13. However, there are some very high/long routes

* *Refer to end of this chapter on how to access video linked with QR code.*

when climbing outdoors, with greater distances between quickdraws. Build up your confidence here too. Remember, just because you feel comfortable falling indoors, you may not do so when on real rock.

If you dedicate a session, or part of a session, to falling practice – don't expect to start from where you left off the next time you put in some practice.

Take it down a few notches, and build it up again. Progress will be much quicker. It can be very beneficial to add fall practice at the start of your climbing session and incorporate this as part of your warm-up. As mentioned previously, if you practice this with a friend, only look at your progress, and prevent yourself from comparing, as this can be very counterproductive.

All this falling practice can be mentally very tiring. So, make sure to give yourself a break, and have some fun climbing. The following are some falling games that you can have fun with and are less structured.

Lary Arce on Huirradica 8a,
El Salto, México
José Mario

FALLING GAMES

With all of the following games, make sure you are high enough off the ground to play these and that there is enough margin for error. If indoors, do not do any of the falling off until the fifth quickdraw is clipped; some exercises may require you to be higher. Also, make sure the route lends itself to falling off, and you are not practising these on a slab or a route with a volume sticking out. Again, some of the exercises are a little more advanced for both belayer and climber, as indicated.

Each of the following exercises are marked with a symbol indicating the level of difficulty for the climber. The three categories are:

Beginner exercise – exercise which can be used for someone who is just starting out to work on their head-game, little experience is needed here.

Intermediate exercise – here the climber needs to be comfortable with lead climbing, and also have some experience working on their head-game, these exercises are on the lower end of pushing the mental boundaries.

Advanced exercise – here the climber needs to be an efficient lead climber. They will need to be comfortable with falling on lead climbing, these exercises are on the higher end of pushing the mental boundaries.

CLIP-DROP

Choose a route that feels easy to climb. Only fall off after you have clipped the fourth quickdraw. Here is where you clip the quickdraw, and as soon as it is clipped, you let go. Practice this on every quickdraw after the fourth one, until the top. You are technically on a top rope, as your waist should be below the last clipped quickdraw. There should be a little slack in the system, and the belayer should prevent taking any in as soon as the quickdraws are clipped.*

* *Refer to end of this chapter on how to access video linked with QR code.*

LAST-DITCH EFFORT

This is a great game to incorporate when either tired or playing on your project. When you feel pumped and don't think you can make the next move, jump and touch the next hold, don't attempt to grab on.

Again, make sure you are high enough off the ground to do so. This game can be played intentionally, with the belayer being aware of this – so he or she can anticipate this. Or this can be incorporated in your general climbing, as the belayer ALWAYS needs to be paying attention.*

BELAYER LED FALLS

This is where the climber and belayer come up with a word, which could be any word, and when the belayer shouts it – the climber has to let go without hesitation. Make sure you agree on a word before setting off. The belayer will have a set amount of falls he/she would like the climber to take (for example, 5). The belayer will add two more falls for each time the climber hesitates.

The belayer must be aware of the climber's comfort zone, learning zone, and the edge of their risk zone. For example, if the climber feels that being above a clip about to clip the next bolt and falling off is too far into their risk zone, the belayer must be aware and not force the climber to fall off there. Build this up. The idea of this game is that you are not always in control, i.e. the equivalent of going to an insecure hold, or an unfamiliar route.*

To bring this game to the next level, you can use this anywhere in your climbing session, where it could be used at any time. So, you have no idea when to expect it. Just make sure you don't use it when someone is trying their project.

* *Refer to end of this chapter on how to access video linked with QR code.*

CLIMBER LED FALLS

Both climber and belayer are aware the game is going to be played. The climber falls off at several different points (anywhere after the fifth or sixth quickdraw, as long as it is safe to do so). As the climber, you cannot communicate with your belayer to tell him/her that you are about to fall off. Also, try not to hang onto a hold in a stationary position whilst building up to let go as the belayer expects you to fall. The idea is that by giving no signals away to the belayer that you are about to fall off, you, as the climber learn to trust that your belayer is always there to catch you and keep you safe. Especially good for people who like being in control. You can build this up slowly.*

TWISTER

Pick a lower off, where there are a selection of routes of varying difficulty (indoor setting).

The belayer is in charge of shouting which colour holds to use. Try and make the route easy, or within the climber's ability up to the fourth clip – then you can up the ante or climb the easier route on the wall up to the 4th quickdraw, then play the game. The belayer shouts a colour; this is the next hold the climber has to use but is not allowed to match. And so on to the top. The idea is that it gets trickier the higher up the climber goes. Before setting off, decide which footholds you are going to use, i.e. hands as feet, any foot, or you pick footholds as well. The idea behind this game is that when on-siting a route, you are not always sure what is coming up, and that element of control is taken away. The belayer's job is getting the climber to fall off higher up; the climber's job is to make it to the top. You can even come up with a forfeit to make it more interesting. It can be helpful here to have a third person shouting the colours the climber has to follow, as it sometimes can be tough to see, as the belayer, where you want the climber to go. Here, knowledge of climbing movements is essential for the belayer.*

** Refer to end of this chapter on how to access video linked with QR code.*

DYNO NINJA

Pick a route of easy/medium difficulty, ideally a slightly overhanging one with big holds.

Pre clip the first four quickdraws, then come back down to the ground. Try and make the biggest moves you possibly can, and see how few holds you can use on a particular route. Again, this is an exercise you can build up over time; this is an excellent game for static climbers or people that lack commitment. If you fall, it doesn't matter; try again. Do this all the way to the top. A fun game to compete with yourself or a friend.*

FINGER NINJA

Pick a lower off with a good selection of holds. Pre-clip the first four quickdraws, then come back down. Here you dynamically move up, release both hands simultaneously and grab two different holds. Make sure you don't forget to clip. Here, of course, you can release one hand. You are not allowed to readjust. You can increase the difficulty if you haven't fallen off; this is a great game for static climbers or people that lack commitment. If you fall, it doesn't matter; try again. Do this all the way to the top.*

CHILLAX MAN!

When on a route, and you feel entirely boxed (pumped) and feel you cannot progress further, stop, close your eyes, and focus on your breathing. Deep slow breathing – close your eyes, focus on the tension you are holding in your body and try to relax as much as possible.

If you need to visualise your happy place, do so. Try and relax and see how long you can hold on. You can try to relax to the point you fall off.*

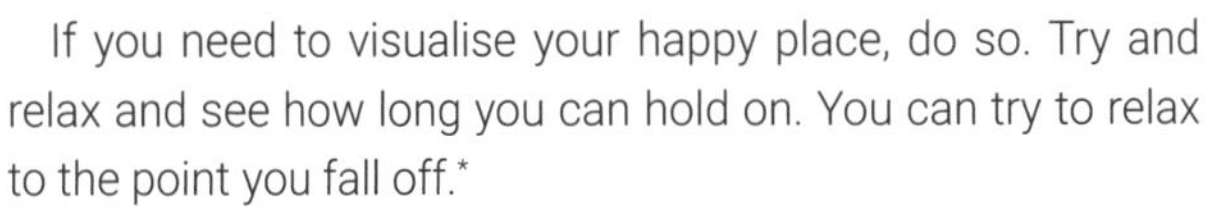

* *Refer to end of this chapter on how to access video linked with QR code.*

FINAL WORD

Have lots of fun playing around with these exercises and games, and build up your confidence slowly.

Progress at the pace of the climber, and be patient. These exercises can be mentally draining, so when you feel you have worked through a number of them. Relax, and have some fun climbing. Get back to them in the next session. And on the days when you feel a little off, accept how you feel and take off the pressure.

COACHES' ADVICE

I often hear or see coaches asking novice climbers to take some large falls. For example, at most climbing walls, when newbies to lead climbing attend a three or four-part course, there will usually be a session that involves falling and catching falls. But why would you ask someone who has never fallen before on lead (or very few unexpected ones) to take a large fall? Their comfort zone, for most, just about getting their heads around the fact that all of the equipment may keep them safe. And the fact that someone else is holding them is a lot to get your head around. We may have this innate drive to climb from a young age, but we definitely do not have a natural comfort with falling.

Being asked by an instructor/coach to take a relatively large fall onto the rope – which the instructors know would work and is safe – may leave a traumatic imprint on the clients' mind as they are psychologically pushed way too far outside their comfort zone. This is counter-productive as it will be harder for them to even look at falling after that.

Some characters will be okay with it, but some will NOT. So why not spend an extra session building up their confidence, PROGRESSIVELY. Taking into account that progressive means different things to different people. As mentioned in chapter 3 (The Learning Zone Model and Optimal Performance Theory), it can take one person fewer falls to become accustomed to falling and someone else more. So, this is where you, as an instructor, need to be very observant of your clients.

There are even lots of instructors who struggle with falling themselves.

What can you do as an instructor?

1. Speak to the client – Ask them what the scariest thing they have done is. That will give you an idea of whether they are an adrenaline junkie or a more cautious person. But here, do not make assumptions that if someone has jumped out of a plane with a parachute, they will be fine falling on a rope.
2. Ask them how they feel? – You may have to ask this question a few times to get the real answer. Try and listen to what they have to say and watch their body language as this can tell you a lot.
3. Progressive falling exercises
4. Equipment – Talk about the climbing equipment's strength, i.e. the rope, the carabiners, the belay loop on the harness, the quickdraws, and its breaking strengths. Talk about how this translates to real-life examples.
5. Reassurance – Explain what will happen and reassure them that all will be well, that you are there to keep them safe. When you think about it, it is a huge thing to entrust someone with your life. As a newbie climber, it certainly feels you are putting yourself in a very vulnerable position, where it feels you give control away to someone else.
6. Instructor's job – Explain that you, as the instructor, are there to hold the dead rope and make sure everything is done safely. Again, this is further reassurance.
7. Belay device – If you are using an assisted braking belay device, explain how this works.

It is vital that as a coach/instructor that you emotionally tune into your clients and that you are aware of their feelings, whether they communicate this with you or not.

Reassure them, and look at progressive falling exercises. Do not expect your clients to take big whippers on their first climbing/falling session. Maybe there are a lot of instructors out there that would struggle with taking big falls. Try to put yourselves in your clients' shoes.

FROM PRACTICE TO REAL FALLS

So, how do we go from taking deliberate practice falls to doing it for real? Again, just like practice falls, is gradual repetition. The importance here is not to try and transition too quickly, from taking practice falls into falling off a route as you are physically unable to hold on or unable to figure out the movement in the moment. That's where we all want to get to, right!?

Depending on the type of person you are, some of us deal better with higher levels of stress, while others prefer lower levels of stress to perform well (see Chapter 3 – IZOF theory). But let's assume that you prefer a gradual transition for the sake of argument. Before we progress to falling off routes naturally, we need to be comfortable with the following:

- Fall practice has to be ingrained into every climbing session
- We need to be relaxed when we fall
- Be comfortable with falling in all different types of scenarios (i.e., above bolt, with slack in hand, etc.), heights and terrain (i.e., overhangs, headwalls, slabs, etc.)
- Comfortable falling without signalling to the belayer we are going to fall (i.e., through shouting "Take", downclimbing, hanging on for a while before deciding to let go, etc.)
- Be aware of our mental processes in climbing and falling and how these may affect our performance (self-awareness)
- Be well-practiced at breathing techniques when stressed

If you choose to transition too quickly, or your mind is not ready, you will find some of your old habits creeping back in, as you are pushing your comfort zone a little too much and may end up operating close or in the panic zone. When you feel ready to make the transition to real falls, follow some of the simple rules as described below:

- Make sure you are mentally in a good place when you practice real falls
- Make sure you are ready for it (i.e., have practiced progressive falling lots)
- Mention to the belayer not to take in when you are climbing (unless you are close to the ground or there is the potential to hit an obstacle)
- Be aware of the game the mind plays; the mind seeks 'safety/comfort', so stay in the moment when the feeling of fear makes an appearance through breathing techniques (see Chapter 8 – Breathing)

Michael Kimber taking air on Ione, 7a, Poets, Kalymnos
📷 Kieran Duncan

- Attempt routes that are a grade or two above your limit
- Start with one move at your physical limit, and slowly build this up (be sure to reward yourself for trying)

Be aware - the mind sometimes struggles to give away control because as we approach our limit, we feel out of control and think we can predict the outcome. You will find your true capability when you leave behind the self-imposed limits. Keep fighting, keep trying, and keep working at it.

Practice, practice, practice, and a lot more PRACTICE.

"Courage is the most important of all virtues, because without courage you can't practice any other virtue consistently. You can practice a virtue erratically, but nothing consistently without courage."
MAYA ANGELOU

*Use your mobile phone in the camera function to scan the QR code. This will take you to a link with a video. The video is password-protected and case sensitive, password is:

Psychology

If you have any problems accessing the QR codes, please email me on info@riseandsummit.co.uk

Tribe (9a on trad – scary), Cardarese, Italy

📷 Pietro Porro

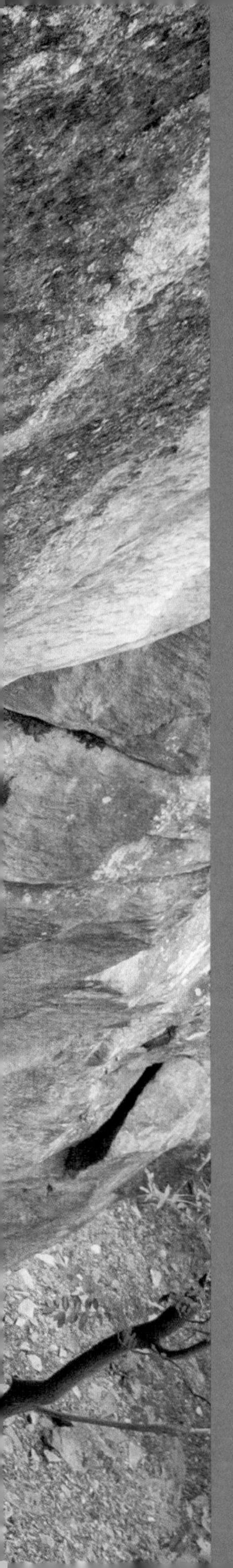

"

CLIMBING TRIBE WAS THE CULMINATION OF A LOT OF THINGS FOR ME.

YEARS OF TRAINING FOR HARD SPORT CLIMBS AND BOULDERS GOT ME PHYSICALLY READY, AND DECADES OF TRAD CLIMBING EXPERIENCE MADE SURE THAT I COULD MAKE THE MOST OF WHATEVER PHYSICAL CAPABILITIES I HAD. VISUALISATION PLAYED A HUGE PART, BOTH IN REHEARSING THE MOVES, BUT ALSO LEARNING TO COPE WITH THE STRESS IN THE MOMENT. THE BIGGEST THING HOWEVER WAS SOMETHING TOTALLY UNEXPECTED. LEARNING TO LET GO. I'VE STRUGGLED A LOT OVER THE YEARS WITH PERFORMANCE PRESSURE AND ANXIETY, SOMETIMES NEEDING FAR LONGER THAN 'I SHOULD HAVE' TO CLIMB A PROJECT, ONLY TO DO IT ON THE DAY WHEN I LEAST EXPECTED. BECOMING A FATHER HAS FINALLY SHOWN ME THAT THE MOST IMPORTANT THING IS NOT TO TRY TOO HARD TO CONTROL EVERYTHING, JUST LET THINGS FLOW, AND ENJOY AND APPRECIATE ALL THE LITTLE MOMENTS ALONG THE WAY.

"

JAMES PEARSON

Diego Ivan López Iturralde smiling on his way down in the Blue Mountains

CHAPTER 12

What Type of Character are You?

"The mountains have rules. They are harsh rules, but they are there, and if you keep to them you are safe. A mountain is not like men. A mountain is sincere. The weapons to conquer it exist inside you, inside your soul."

WALTER BONATTI

This chapter is a bit tongue in cheek. Categorising each type of climber with their behavioural traits. You may have characteristics of several of the described personalities. In this chapter, character types are described, and useful games are suggested that can be played to increase confidence.

THE STATIC CLIMBER

This climber loves to make each move statically; they are usually very strong because they love hanging on and cranking. They love security.

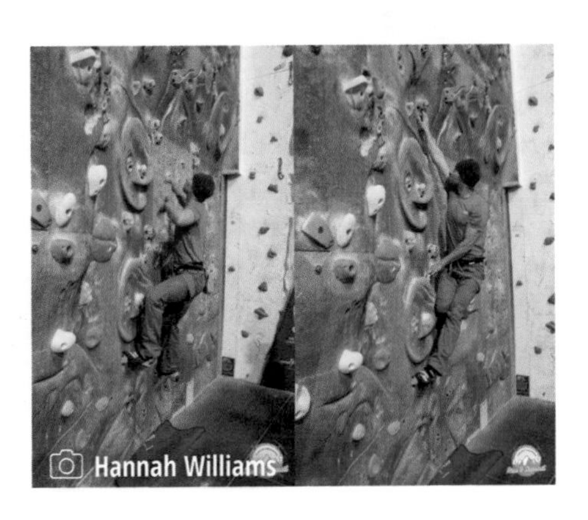
Hannah Williams

Games/exercises: belayer led falls, dyno ninja, twister (belayer makes sure some of the moves have to be made dynamically), last-ditch effort

THE HESITATOR (NON-COMMITTER)

This climber loves to move up and down the same hold many times before committing to the next hold. By either hanging on too long or making small micro-movements without going anywhere, wasting energy whilst doing so; this can sometimes be because of the inner critic we have within us, telling us we're not going to make it.

This climber also dislikes moving to a potentially insecure hold because they do not like the insecurity of something they think they cannot hold. But how would you know if you are not on that hold yet?

They sometimes struggle to see they can make the next move, so they decide to downclimb five moves to 'safety'.

Hannah Williams

Games/exercises: belayer led falls, finger ninja, last-ditch effort

THE OVER-GRIPPER

Maybe you over-grip on routes, as the possibility of falling off increases. If you are an over-gripper, try, when you get halfway up a route (and it is safe to fall off), to close your eyes, do some deep belly breathing, and try and relax. Think about the tension in your body, especially your arms, and see how much tension (i.e. your grip and shoulders) you can release before falling off. In some situations, you will be able to release enough to increase the blood flow to your forearms, allowing them to regenerate.

Hannah Williams

Over-gripping can also be related to a lack of trust in the equipment or belayer. Looking at progressive falling exercises will certainly help too.

Games/exercises: Chillax man!, climber led falls, progressive falling exercises, last-ditch effort

THE NONBELIEVER (IN ONESELF)

This climber has a lot of negative talk going around in his/her head. They are very good at self-criticism, worrying, comparing themselves to others, or talk negatively about themselves. They talk themselves out of attempting a project that deep inside they would love to try. They may focus on their worries whilst climbing and only focus on the negatives.

Mike Chrimes

Games/exercises:

- Pick out anything done positively when climbing (here, the belayer can help, but ideally, the climber needs to name anything they have done well on each route they climb)
- Forget about the negatives, do not think about these
- Pick achievable steps, and affirm once completed
- Breathing
- Performance anxiety routine (see next chapter)
- Progressive falling exercises
- Using a wall chart to keep track of progress over time
- Belayer led falls
- Twister
- Tell your belayer the route you feel you would like to climb but can't. With a little encouragement over time, get on the route, climb up to a certain height, to the point you feel it is manageable, then come down. The next time, try one more move, even if you just hang around there and play around with breathing exercises. Build this up over time and see what happens. Keep track of your progress.

THE SYSTEM DOUBTER (OR ENGINEER)

This is the person that doubts the equipment and whether it may work as intended. They may even look at the few strands of a fluffy sheath (that happens with regular wear) and panic that it may not hold.

Mike Chrimes

All of the equipment you have for climbing is designed to take tremendous forces. All designed to a very high standard and unlikely to ever experience their full capacity. All of your climbing equipment has a strength rating marked in kN (kilo Newtons). 1kN equates to 100Kg of force.

- Dynamic climbing rope – these are designed to withstand a minimum force of 18kN. As climbing ropes are dynamic, a falling climber will never produce this kind of force in any normal climbing situation. Most climbing falls generate around 5kN (again, this depends on the amount of rope out and the distance the climber falls)
- Locking carabiner – these are designed to take a minimum load of 20kN but are usually able to withstand forces of 23kN upwards.
- Quickdraw – these are designed to take forces with the snap gate open and closed, ranging from 8–9kN when open to 22–25kN when closed.
- Strength of belay loop – the belay loop has to withstand 15kN for 3 minutes to pass European standards, but most manufacturers will design these to withstand higher forces.

Games/exercises: progressive falling exercises, clip-drop, last-ditch effort

THE CONTROLLER

This is the climber that struggles to hand over control of holding the rope to someone else.

Hannah Williams

Whilst climbing, they may look down to check the belayer is paying attention and holding the rope, or suggest to take in more rope to the belayer as they are climbing up on the route. They may check the belayer's belay device and feel uncertain when they pull out an ATC.

Here the climber needs to slowly build up confidence with the belayer, and take progressive falls without the belayer knowing as this builds confidence that the belayer is able to do their job and keep them safe. Once confidence is high, try and play the climber led falling game (see the previous chapter).

If it is the first time the belayer and climber are in partnership, ask a (competent) friend to check their belaying. There is usually a floorwalker (i.e. qualified instructor) in climbing centres who would be happy to check, just to put your mind at ease.

Games/exercises: Climber led falls, last-ditch effort

THE AVOIDER (WILL AVOID GOING TO THE LIMIT)

Here, the climber will have a great desire to climb something at their physical or psychological limit, but will give into to their anxiety, and avoid this at any cost. Or they would climb a route; then when they get to a part of the climb, where they think they will fall off, they either downclimb to a clip, hold the rope or shout "Take", i.e. moving back to comfort.

Mike Chrimes

Games/exercises:

- Progressive falling exercises
- Climb a route that you think is outside of your comfort zone, then when the usual pattern would be downclimbing, stop, focus on belly breathing, or focus on something else, even just stay in that position, try to relax best you can. Just by delaying the process of the usual pattern you follow, you are putting in change.
- When on the floor, ask the belayer not to take in, when on a route as the climber you may say, in a moment of stress, 'take'.
- Belayer led falls
- Last-ditch effort

THE SPACE AVOIDER

As the name states, this climber will avoid routes with an overhang, as they feel uncomfortable with all of that space below them, although it is much safer to fall here as there are no obstacles to hit on the way down. Or they will climb the routes, but stress levels will increase the closer they get to the overhang, where they may over-grip, then rest, or downclimb to safety.

Mike Chrimes

Games/exercises:

- Slowly building up confidence on an overhang.
- Climb up to overhang, no further.
- Until comfortable, then one more quickdraw or move on the overhang, etc. Build this up over time.
- Progressive falling exercises on overhanging terrain
- Climb lots of easy routes on the overhanging wall

THE I'M-SCARED-OF-FAILURE-SO-I'M-GONNA-CLIMB-SOMETHING-I-KNOW-I-CAN-DO CLIMBER

This climber will avoid any situation where they think they may fail. They will only climb what they know they can. They worry about how others perceive them and state that they will likely fail if they try something they are unsure of.

Mike Chrimes

This climber has a lot of negative talk going around in his/her head. They are very good at self-criticism and comparing themselves to others. They talk themselves out of attempting a project.

Climbing is about a successive sequence of what we call 'failures' to conquer a route.

Phrased differently, it is a sequence of learning steps and figuring out how to complete the route.

Games/exercises:

- Pick achievable steps, and affirm once completed
- Breathing
- Performance anxiety routine (see next chapter)
- Progressive falling exercises
- Using a wall chart to keep track of progress over time
- Belayer led falls
- Twister
- Tell your belayer the route you feel you would like to climb but can't. With a little encouragement over time, get on the route, climb up to a certain height, to the point you feel it is manageable, then come down. The next time, try one more move, even if you just hang around there and play around with breathing exercises. Build this up over time and see what happens. Keep track of your progress.
- Chillax man!

Une Jolie Fleur dans une peau de vache (8b), Alpes des Haute Provence, France

Raph Fourau

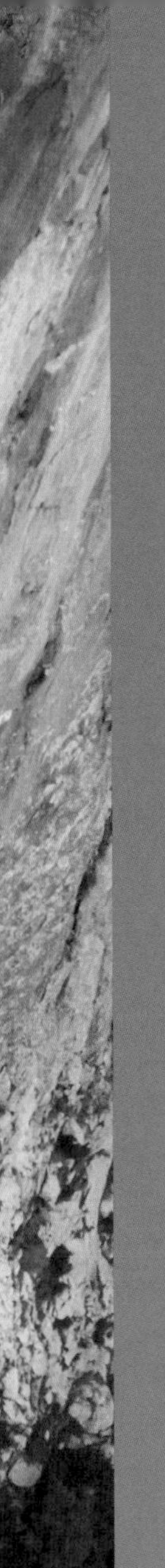

“

A FEW YEARS AGO YUJI HIRAYAMA TOLD ME THAT BEFORE TRYING TO ONSIGHT SALATHÉ HE HAD BEEN VISUALISING FOR A YEAR, TRYING TO IMAGINE HOW IT WOULD FEEL, HOW HE WOULD HANDLE THE FATIGUE...

SO WHEN I BEGAN MY NEXT LONG TERM PROJECT – AT THE TIME IT WAS ‘THE VOIE PETIT’ – I TRIED TO APPLY THAT CONCEPT TO MY ROUTE. EVERY MORNING FOR A FULL YEAR, I WOULD TAKE FIVE MINUTES WHEN I WOKE UP TO IMAGINE A LITTLE SECTION, IMAGINE HOW IT WOULD FEEL TO BE ON THE LAST BELAY, TIRED BUT GATHERING MY ENERGY TO FINISH. IT GETS MUCH EASIER TO IMAGINE ONCE YOU HAVE BEEN ON THE ROUTE. SO FOR ‘UNE JOLIE FLEUR DANS UNE PEAU DE VACHE’, I DID VISUALISE A LOT STANDING AT THE BOTTOM OF THE LAST 8A, GATHERING EVERYTHING THAT I HAD LEFT FOR THE LAST LONG ENDURANCE FIGHT THAT WOULD CONCLUDE THE ROUTE, AND ALSO ALLOWING MYSELF THE RIGHT TO FAIL. ACCEPTING THIS POSSIBILITY, REALISING THAT IT WOULDN’T CHANGE MY LIFE DOES REALLY TAKE AWAY THE PRESSURE. ON THE DAY OF THE ASCENT ALL THIS PREPARATION HELPED A LOT. MY EMOTIONS WERE ALREADY CHANNELLED, I KNEW WHAT I NEEDED TO DO!

”

CAROLINE CIAVALDINI

Climber competing in the Winter Comp at the Warehouse Climbing Centre
Mike Chrimes

CHAPTER 13

Performance Anxiety

"What advantages do we hope to gain (from climbing mountains)? Naturally, there is the pleasure we get from the climbing process itself and our victories, but as well as the delights of exercise in a mountain environment, there is also the process, coming every time as a surprise, of self-discovery deepening a little further with every climb: who we are, how far we can go, what is our potential, where are the limits of our technique, our strength, our skill, our mountaineering sense: discoveries whose acceptance means that, if necessary, we may turn back and return another time, several times if need be- 'Tomorrow is a new day.' "

GASTON REBUFFAT

David is quietly sat in the lecture hall. The nerves ever-rising, with the knowledge that his presentation is up next. His senses numbed with anxiety, his breathing short and fast, he's trying to wipe off the sweat from his hands onto his trousers.

Every time he does more appears.

"Pointless", he thinks. The lecturer calls his name. Phased out with anxiety, David cannot hear until the lecturer touches him on the shoulder. As if awoken from deep meditation, he shakes his head, takes a deep breath, and sets off on that lonely walk to the front of the class, like a lamb to slaughter. A darkness came over him, with the realisation 342 pairs of eyes were watching him.

With his mind blank and the intensity of the onlooking eyes, he stutters his first few lines.

The room bursts out laughing.

David is trying to remind himself how to manage his feelings. He remembers a friend telling him to imagine the audience naked; it always works for his friend. A long silence, as he is trying, nothing. He then decides to continue with what he prepared, and finally, David starts to relax.

We have all flunked a presentation or job interview at some point in our lives. The pressure and anxiety have been too much to deal with; fast heart rate, blank minds, messed up lines in a play.

Performance anxiety is the fear of one's ability to perform a specific task under self-imposed pressure. The stress arises from the difference in the perception of the demands placed upon us and our perceived ability to cope with those demands. The fear may be related to falling off a route or not doing as well as hoped. It is the worry of not performing well due to not knowing the future outcome. So, as we discussed in chapter 6 (The influence of thought), it is a normal human feeling, and we all do it to varying degrees. If we feel able to cope with the demands placed upon us, then we are likely to feel lower levels of

Long Duong on Chain Reaction (5.12c), Smith Rock
Todd Tang

stress. Anxiety or fear, usually arise when we perceive the demands placed upon us to be greater than our perceived ability to cope with those demands.

Performance anxiety does not only occur when competing; it can happen in every climbing session. The pressure you feel to perform, self-imposed or not.

Psychologically, we focus on our worry and may not climb in a flow state (Chapter 4 – Normal zone and flow zone). Physiologically, the body releases epinephrine (adrenaline), which increases your heart rate, respiratory rate, and raises your blood sugar levels. Also, some of your muscles may tense up. Here, there is a greater probability of not climbing efficiently, using more energy where it is not needed, especially with breathing and the heart rate rising; this can vary from mild nervousness to higher anxiety levels.

Let's first look at anxiety.

ANXIETY

If we look at the definition of anxiety, it means "a feeling of worry, nervousness, or unease about something with an uncertain outcome". For example, the feeling you feel before attempting your project or as you are about to compete. As described in chapter 3 on the catastrophe model, anxiety can take many forms. We have state, trait, cognitive, and somatic anxiety.

- State anxiety – is the anxiety felt in a given situation
- Trait anxiety – is part of an individual's personality, a predisposition due to personality traits, the influence of parents, and experiences
- Cognitive anxiety – refers to the negative thoughts, worries, doubts, or concerns someone may experience
- Somatic anxiety – relates to the physiological symptoms brought on by high pressure moments, i.e., butterflies, trembling, shortness of breath, etc.

How does anxiety differ from fear? The difference is that anxiety is a generalised response to an unknown threat or internal conflict, whereas fear is focused on a known external danger. Although both can have the same physiological responses (see Chapter 1 – Fear and the Brain), like fear, anxiety can kick start the sympathetic nervous system, namely the fight-or-flight response.

CAUSES AND SYMPTOMS OF ANXIETY

Anxiety arises when we perceive the demands placed upon us to be greater than the perceived ability to cope with those demands. When both cognitive and somatic anxiety is excessive, these will affect performance. Whether we are attempting our project, a route where we know we may experience fear, or competing. Some of the following topics can influence our performance anxiety levels.

- Born with higher levels of anxiety (trait) – you may have higher levels of trait anxiety, which causes you to be more sensitive to anxiety-provoking situations.
- Trauma – you may have experienced trauma/traumatic event, which has caused you to be more anxious or experience higher levels of anxiety given a certain situation.
- Concerned for an outcome – worrying about the outcome of your performance can create high levels of anxiety, which can hinder performance.
- The expectation of performance – whether this is self-imposed pressure or from an external force (e.g., coach, parents, etc.), this pressure can create anxiety and prevent you from climbing fluidly.
- Perfectionist – a perfectionist will have high expectations, may fear failure, and will tend to be outcome focused. All of which can create high levels of anxiety.
- Negative thinking – see chapter 6 (The influence of thought).
- Fear of failing – people who fear "failure" will tend to have higher levels of anxiety, given the pressure they put upon themselves to perform. See chapter 5 (Failure and growth mindset).
- Social acceptance – we may be concerned with how we look or how we are perceived by others. The anxiety of our self-image.
- Inability to deal with uncertainty or adversity – we may have low mental resilience or toughness, which can cause our self-confidence to be low, especially when we experience "failure" or think we may experience failure.
- Problems with focusing – this can be the result of a hormonal imbalance (not just referring to the ladies, men can also experience hormonal imbalances due to a variety of reasons), being too much outside your comfort zone, your levels of anxiety are high, or not practiced enough at focusing. The lack of focus can create performance anxiety.
- Critical of self – this can often lead to higher levels of anxiety, fear of failure, stress, and avoidance of new experiences.

- Past performance can shape how we perceive ourselves to be, shaping our self-image and affecting future performance. For example, the last two times Joe attempted a 7a (5.11d – physical limit), he messed up the start as the nerves got too high. This could shape his self-belief about his future performances when he attempts a 7a.
- Doubt in own ability – through lack of self-confidence or belief, or basing our future self on past poor performances.
- A new challenge – like the first time you attempt a route difficulty above your limit or on unfamiliar terrain, the unknown can also induce anxiety.

These are just a few examples of aspects that may affect performance anxiety. Performance anxiety is normal, especially in situations in which we attach importance. Higher than normal levels of anxiety can have the following effects on one:

- Indecision
- Loss of confidence
- Poor concentration
- Images of failure
- Thoughts of avoidance
- Focused on the wrong part of our performance instead of being in the moment
- Muscular tension
- Levels of arousal too high (see Chapter 3 – Optimal Performance theory)
- Losing your nerve under pressure (choking)
- Avoidance

So where do we need to be? Too relaxed or extremely aroused? When climbing, we need to be somewhere between these two extremes to perform at our best. However, this depends on how you perform, as an individual, according to Hanin's Individual Zone of Optimal Functioning theory (as described in Chapter 3 – The learning Zone model and optimal performance theory).

Anxiety can be viewed as a negative, but it can also positively affect performance and drive one to perform better. Therefore, each person has his/her own preferred level of anxiety that allows them to perform at their best. This is where building self-awareness can come in handy. Put yourself in different situations, notice how you feel, and note how you perform.

Let's look at ways we can manage that anxiety.

MANAGING ANXIETY

So, depending on the type of person you are, if anxiety affects your performance negatively, you need to clear your mind and be as relaxed as possible to climb more efficiently.

For example, we can use a specific climbing routine or mental rehearsal before we set off on our climb. Personally, I will use a routine on most climbs, even some of the easier ones - a mental rehearsal for when the climbing requires any effort.

"If your dreams don't scare you, they are not big enough"
MOHAMMED ALI

Research shows that there are performance benefits to pre-performance routines and mental rehearsals.

Increasing relaxation, lowering stress hormones, and improving attention, emotional stability, and confidence. It also helps clear the mind.

What can really help here is finding out your own emotion profiling results of the exercise you completed (see Chapter 3 – emotion profiling exercise). If you haven't done that, do that.

On the opposite page are some examples of how we can manage our performance anxiety when we climb.

Ron Lach

MENTAL REHEARSAL

Adam Ondra is lying on the floor of the Flatanger cave. A sport climbing venue, secretly hidden away in one of Norway's countless Fjords, made famous by Adam's challenging first ascents. Currently, the area is home to 20 routes of grade 9a and above, mostly first ascents by Adam.

With the 80m flawless slab of granite towering over him and the help of Klaus Isele, an Austrian physiotherapist and osteopath, Adam is going through his visualisation process to climb 'Silence', a 9c project - Imagining himself climbing each of the moves.

Klaus is helping Adam immerse himself completely. Adam visualises the movements and clipping positions. Klaus is holding Adam's hands and feet to create pressure, mimicking the feeling of each of the moves. Adam envisages the effort he has to exert, the breathing, the rests, where to shake out and chalk up. A 3-D all-encompassing process. To a bystander, it could look like Adam is having a seizure, but it is an essential process for Adam's ascent of Silence, the first 9c in the world.

"The more you visualise, the more you have it dialled and the easier the route feels," Adam states.

He feels it helps him build muscle memory and stick those more challenging moves - preventing hesitation and making the whole process of the actual climbing feel autonomous.

Mental rehearsal refers to visualisation – imagining the feelings and sensations of the performance. It is a way of managing emotions and stress under pressure, whether competing or aiming to complete your project. It can aid the athlete in achieving a state of relaxation. A routine practised by many athletes and students preparing for a presentation, individuals preparing for a job interview, or even approaching a difficult subject with a partner, friend or family member.

Within climbing, this can be from climbing movements, the way that holds are to be held, clipping positions, or footwork. It is all part of the route reading process. Some people refer to it as the climbing dance. Surely you have witnessed, if not participated, in this dance. Climbers are stood on the floor, mimicking the movements on the floor of the route they are about to climb.

You can even incorporate how you may feel on the route, especially the crux section or a section where you may feel scared. Visualise your feelings and your coping mechanisms on a difficult part. The mental rehearsal can help reduce the mental noise we have when climbing, enabling us to concentrate on the task at hand.

As we develop our mental rehearsal process, we should think about our senses.

Apart from visualising the route or the movements, we need to think about how we may feel on the crux or the part where we may fall off. Think about what you may experience - anxiety, fear, insecurity. How will you deal with the described feelings, and what may the outcome be?

Studies by Cox (1986), Minas (1978), and Ryan (1981), to name a few, have proven that mental rehearsal can greatly benefit performance. Neural learning in the brain creates a sense of muscle memory and mobilises the subconscious mind, providing the ability to solve routes efficiently.

PETTLEP model

Holmes and Collins (2001) formulated the PETTLEP model, a set of practical guidelines to help devise the visualisation process. PETTLEP is an acronym, where each letter represents an important part of the imagery process to consider:

P	Physical
E	Environment
T	Task
T	Timing
L	Learning
E	Emotion
P	Perceptive

Table 13.1 Components of PETTLEP model

Physical – This is the most important component of the process of imagery. Instead of only visualising the process (i.e., the climb), the more physical you can make the process, the more optimal the benefits, just like when Adam did when he was visualising the route 'Silence' with the help of Klaus. Research has shown that the more detailed the imagery process (in the physical sense/movement), the more effective it is in benefiting performance (Smith et al., 2001).

Environment – This relates to the place where imagery is performed. The PETTLEP states this should be as similar as possible to the performance environment or in the actual performance arena (Smith et al., 2007), which in this case would be the climbing centre or crag you are looking to climb, to develop the greatest benefits. Of course, suppose this is not a practical option. In that case, the use of video and audio may be useful in aiding mental simulation of the venue, i.e., a video of you or someone else climbing your project or even a video of the environment you are looking to climb in.

Task – The imagery should be appropriate to your skill level and your personal preferences as the athlete. As a 6a (5.10a) climber, you would not attempt to visualise climbing 'La Dura Dura' (9b+/5.15c), as I imagine it is a little too far outside your skill level. The content of the imagery needs to be specific to the performer. If you are a coach, it can be very useful to quiz the athlete regarding his or her focus during performance when planning the imagery.

Timing – This refers to the speed at which imagery is completed. It is suggested that the athlete performs the imagery in real time to achieve the greatest benefits. Slow-motion imagery can be used to perfect some of the smaller details in climbing movement, but more research needs to be done on this area.

Learning – This part of the process emphasises that the content of the imagery should be adapted in response to learning. Meaning that if your physical condition, skill level, physical fitness, or emotional ability to cope with segments of fear/stress on the route, this progress should all be incorporated into the visualisation process to enhance performance.

Emotion – The imagery process needs to reflect the emotional experience one feels in their performance, leading to a truer reflection of the actual experience, leading to greater muscle activation (Wilson, Smith, Holmes and Burden – 2010). Smith et al. (2007) found that preceding the imagery process with relaxation is more effective.

Perspective – This refers to the viewpoint of the performer during imagery. This can be internal (through the eyes of the performer) or external (seeing oneself performing as if watching on tv). This depends on your preference, so if you are unsure, play around with both.

The research suggests that you use each component of the PETTLEP model to get the best results, incorporating all of your senses. Next time you go climbing, have a go at this process, and slowly over time, try and add more complexity to the mental rehearsal process. Start with hand movements, then foot movements, clipping positions, the effort required to make certain moves, rest positions, feelings and emotions on the crux, and coping mechanisms. I'm not saying do what Adam Ondra does on every climb you attempt, but why not if it helps.

Make sure you personalise the process, get creative and be innovative.

SELF-HYPNOSIS

Self-hypnosis is a state of heightened awareness and relaxation that is self-induced. In sports performance, this is sometimes combined with imagery. Many athletes use it to manage the feeling of stress and induce a state of relaxation.

There is a feeling of scepticism surrounding this subject that is used a lot in Eastern culture.

Whether it is the Tibetan monks meditating to enlightenment or the Yogi's transcendental meditation into relaxation and self-development, an art form practised over the centuries.

"The eyes of the heart" is one of the Samurais "Twelve rules of the Sword" - This is a form of self-hypnosis whereby a Samurai requires his heart and eyes are connected before a battle; otherwise, if his mind is elsewhere, he is likely to have met his fate.

Please try the following exercise, taken from Dan Millman's book, 'Body, Mind, Mastery'.

DEEP RELAXATION EXERCISE

Lie on your back on a carpet or mattress, and loosen any tight clothing. Have a friend read the following instructions or record them on your phone and play them to yourself. Once you know the steps and your body gets accustomed to this state, you can easily go through the process at any time, even in a few minutes.

Be aware of the body's weight. Breathing slowly and naturally, surrender to gravity. Notice the floor pressing up against the body and the body pressing equally down into the floor.

Put your attention on your feet - imagine they are very heavy. Feel the skin heavy, the bones heavy, the whole body becoming heavy.

Feel the deep, profound heaviness spreading up into your lower legs and through the knees, releasing all of the muscles.

Feel the lower legs heavy, the shin heavy, the bones heavy, the whole body becoming heavy.

Let the pleasant heaviness sink deep into the lower back - releasing - and continue into the upper back, around and under the shoulder blades, along

the spine - releasing - heavy. Let the upper back and neck muscles sink into gravity's pull - skin heavy, bones heavy - the whole body - heavy.
Let go of the upper arms - the elbows and the lower arms - feel the heaviness all the way to the fingertips - skin, bones - the whole body - heavy.
Feel all the neck muscles - front, back, and sides - release and sink to the floor - skin, bones - the whole body - heavy.
Now the entire body below the neck is heavy, totally relaxed. If you feel any tension anywhere, let it go and become twice as heavy.
Now, as I name the areas of the face and scalp, feel them as heavy, and let them go with gravity - skin, bones - the whole body - heavy.
Feel the scalp release - all the muscles of the forehead - around the eye sockets - the cheeks, letting go - the muscles around the nose - the mouth and jaw, releasing - the chin, and around the ears.
Now your entire body is in deep relaxation. Energies flow through the body freely, revitalising, healing, rebalancing.
Notice your breathing. Imagine you're floating gently on your own warm, private ocean.
As you inhale, feel yourself float slowly up, and on exhalation, float back down - experience the well-being of total relaxation.
Imagine the blood coursing freely through the body, nourishing it. Feel the energy of the body vibrating within the cells.
Feel the peacefulness of relaxation. Notice how calm the mind is at the moment – and how open your feelings are. Now begin to increase the depth of your breathing. Ending with three gigantic breaths of energy, open your eyes, and sit up.
Stretch like a cat.

Some of you are sceptics, and I know what you are thinking as that's what I thought as well. Please try the exercise, even if it is only once, and notice the difference in how you feel.

I am not saying that every time you climb, you need to go through this whole exercise, but you can take the idea of this self-hypnosis exercise and make your own.

The idea is that we take some time to breathe, relax, and lower any feelings of stress.

BREATHING

As we looked at in Chapter 8, breathing is the motherboard of the autonomic nervous system. Through slow, deep, rhythmic diaphragmic (belly) breathing, we can kick start the Parasympathetic nervous system (PSNS) and encourage feelings of calm and rest when nervous, anxious, or fearful (refer to Chapter 8 for breathing techniques), as well as through the Vagus nerve. 75% of the Vagus nerve's function is associated with the PSNS, connecting your heart, lungs, and other vital organs.

The Vagus nerve responds to one's breathing rate. When our breathing rate slows, the Vagus nerve tells the heart to slow down to match. Stimulating the Vagus nerve directly will have this effect on the heart, which in turn calms down and relaxes our entire body, dropping our heart rate. This trends all the way up through the brain, reducing cortisol and other stress hormones. It is the longer exhale that triggers associated nerves that activate the relaxation response, and it's during the exhale that your Vagus nerve is most active.

We can tone the vagal nerve through regular breathing practice; although some of us may have a genetic predisposition, you can boost it. All it takes is regular practice throughout the day. Deep rhythmic belly breathing and slow long exhales will improve the Vagus nerve's tone and hence benefit your parasympathetic nervous system. Find the time when you wake up, throughout the day, and when you go to bed. So that when it comes to climbing, your system is well practiced, and it comes easy.

OTHER STRATEGIES

There are plenty of other strategies used to help with performance anxiety. Listening to music can help lower your cortisol levels and helps take the edge off the fight-flight response. Music can influence some of the biological processes in the body, like lowering your heartbeat, as long as you listen to music at 60-80bpm, and even produce dopamine (a reward chemical that increases alertness and improves focus). Even singing and dancing can help reduce your stress levels. So next time, stick your headphones on, sing along. Maybe even have a boogie before you set off.

Another coping strategy may be regular Yoga practice. Maybe not something to do in the moment, but if you practice Yoga regularly, you will be looking at breathing techniques (as we have seen has great benefits), strengthening your mind-body connection, and promoting a deeper sense of self-awareness. As we have seen in the book so far, this is a definite must. Research has shown

Ron Lach

that regular Yogis protect the Hippocampus from deteriorating, a part of the brain that helps manage emotions. Yoga's combination of exercise, breathing, and meditation helps create a better mood and a sense of calmness, reducing anxiety and stress.

Or we can increase our body's endorphin (pain reliever) levels. Tiny tears in the muscle fibres create mild pain needed to trigger the release of pain-relieving endorphins in the body. This can be done by stretching or vigorous exercise. Although, research suggests doing dynamic stretching as a warm-up before an event, as static stretching will cause you to lose force and power output. As well as endorphins relieving pain, these help lower anxiety levels. Or a quick burst of vigorous exercise will help lower the levels of anxiety you may be feeling. Just make sure these do not interfere with your performance.

Studies concerning exercise and anxiety confirm the value of incorporating cardiovascular activity as a part of state anxiety resolution.

The study showed that twenty minutes of cardiovascular activity at seventy percent of able capacity resulted in a reduction in anxiety levels similar to that achieved through meditation.

Because different personalities need different levels of stimulation, the exercise routine should be chosen based on individual needs, as a mismatched regimen can contribute to stress rather than alleviate it.

Nutrition is a topic sometimes overlooked. If blood sugars are low, the body responds by showing symptoms such as getting a headache, having cold extremities, or feeling jittery, tired, irritable, anxious, depressed, or unable to concentrate. The body considers this a state of emergency, as if it is being starved, so adrenaline is released as well, creating a faster heart rate and feelings of restlessness. So, make sure you eat before climbing or have regular snacks.

As described in Chapter 6 (The Influence of Thought), positive self-talk can greatly reduce anxiety by boosting motivation and directing attention to where it is needed in the performance. If you find your self-talk is anxious or negative leading up to your performance, notice these thoughts and remind yourself, "These are just thoughts." We all have them. These can be more prevalent when the outcome is unknown, or an event is important to us. Shift your attention away from the end goal, and focus on the now.

Another useful strategy that can be used to manage anxiety and emotions, especially in a competitive environment, is to replicate the environment the best you can in training. For example, the route setting, other competitors, the timings, etc. Some sports now even use Virtual Reality to mimic the stresses of competition.

PRE-PERFORMANCE ROUTINE

> *He carefully places the oval-shaped rugby ball on a kicking tee, aimed between the two posts, makes some minor adjustments, like an interior designer meticulously adjusting the vase on a countertop or an obsessive perfectionist aligning a glass with the pattern on the tablecloth. He takes a few steps back, turns 90 degrees, and takes a few more. Standing in his famous 'Jonny Wilkinson' pose, clasping his hands as if praying to the gods. He takes a few deep breaths and tries to exhale all of his anxieties as he blows out.*
>
> *His concentration intensifies and blocks out the ever excitable and impatient crowd. Jonny Wilkinson is ranked one of the better kickers in the world to this day. He performed this routine every time he tried for a conversion or penalty kick.*

Psychologist Aidan Moran defined a pre-performance routine as 'a sequence of task-relevant thoughts and actions which an athlete engages in systematically before his or her performance of a specific sports skill'. These help the athlete calm their nerves and help focus their concentration on the task at hand.

Here we are not talking about athletes with superstitious behaviours where psychological aids attribute to the placebo effect, which gives a greater sense of control and mental reassurance in a given situation. Like Michael Jordan's lucky shorts he would wear on every game, to Tiger Wood's lucky red shirt, or the kissing of a necklace before taking a penalty kick by some of the famous footballers. Although some studies have proven these can aid performance (Schippers and Van Lange – 2006; Damisch, Stoberock and Mussweiler – 2010).

A pre-performance routine aims to calm the nerves and focus concentration on the task at hand and reduce mental noise.

If I'm looking to attempt a project of mine or climb a route at or near my limit (as my anxiety levels are higher here), I start with the climber's dance, route reading (mental rehearsal). When I feel I have read most or all of the route (this depends on how much is visible, have the ability to work out the moves, or have the moves dialled in my head from having climbed the route repeatedly), I tie in, put shoes on, and get the belayer to check the knot attached to my harness.

I find this step very important, as my anxiety levels are a little higher; it gives me the confidence that someone else has checked my knot - something less to worry about when I'm higher up. Not that I don't trust myself, but I may have gotten distracted as I'm thinking about the sequence of moves on the crux of the climb. I have been climbing for a long time; this part has become so ingrained that I feel naked when this process is missed from my routine.

I then stand in front of the wall/rockface, look at the wall in front or down at the floor, chalk up my hands, shake out my hands, arms and shoulders, whilst taking 2-3 slow deep breaths (to clear the mind and try to relax, a form of self-hypnosis) then start. I do not look up whilst standing in front of the wall/rockface. I have already route read, and I do not need to think about what's above.

I then start climbing.

For me, this routine helps me relax as best I can and focus on the task at hand.

Apart from the obvious parts of my routine that every climber will have to perform anyway, i.e. putting on shoes, tying in, route reading - choose what other elements you add. For me, deep and slow breathing, as we learned in one of the earlier chapters, causes the body to relax and create more energy. Looking down

at the floor keeps my mind away from focusing on any element of the climb that may make me a little more nervous (i.e. harder moves, areas where I keep falling off) - keeping my mind in the present. I look up and start climbing; I am only focusing on the next move, staying in the present as much as possible.
How can you come up with your own routine?

Here are a few pointers in establishing your routine:

- Play around with different elements and sequences
- It may take time to establish a routine, so stick with it
- Your routine will be very individual to you
- Consistency is key – try it on easier routes, and build this up
- Maybe you already have a routine or elements you perform subconsciously
- Always make time for your routine, and if it goes wrong, start again

Remember that you will need to think about how to get to a more relaxed state and a focused mindset in your routine. Maybe you are a climber that prefers to get psyched up before attempting your project.

The following elements can be taken into account and added to your routine:

- Visualisation/mental rehearsal – whether this is route reading, climbing movements, clipping positions, or the feeling of successful climbing, etc. It is vital here to focus on the positives.
- Breathing
- Self-hypnosis
- Listening to your favourite music or music that gets you psyched up just before performing (for me, that could be The Prodigy, as an example. You can always add in a little dance routine).
- Or come up with your own ideas, and let me know what works for you.

Just remember, a pre-performance routine will help you get in 'the zone' quicker, lower your stress levels, and help you get focused, but it will not get rid of all of the nerves.

Fionn Claydon

FINAL WORD

When performing at your limit, whether at a competition or for yourself, it is normal to feel nervous and have butterflies in your stomach. Play around with the techniques described above, and see what works for you. Just trying these once may not help you. Try and incorporate these into your climbing sessions, and see how you can make these your own.

Have fun playing around with these, and happy climbing.

"Winning is only secondary to continuous learning and improvement, focus on the Journey"

Afterword

There is a lot of information contained in this book. The idea is that you become aware of how your mind works and what you can do to change any lifelong habits you may have within climbing.

The change needs to come from within and a drive to make changes in your behaviour – this may feel uncomfortable at times, but stick with it; progress will happen as long as you put in purposeful practice.

Firstly, create an awareness of your behaviour and emotions in and outside of climbing.

Don't anticipate immediate changes – expect to work on these over a long period of time. As you would training on the physical part of climbing, these adaptive changes happen a little at a time, as does the mind.

There is no substitute for purposeful practice, lots of it. Be kind to yourself. Be patient.

Use positive language to describe yourself. Respond to adversity by perceiving it as a challenge. Believe in yourself. Find inspiration in the smallest of changes. Embrace the process of continual learning. And lastly...

make sure you have fun climbing.

For anyone that may be interested, when we recorded some of the footage linked with the book, we had a few mishaps, here are the outtakes.*

*Use your mobile phone in the camera function to scan the QR code. This will take you to a link with a video. The video is password-protected and case sensitive, password is:

Psychology

Acknowledgement

Thanks to my wife Carrie, who has supported me in making my passion my full-time job. And for giving me two beautiful kids, who have made me realise what's important in life, and point out my flaws daily.

To my parents for giving me opportunities to learn, allowing me to beat my own fears in my own time, always being there whether a grazed knee or broken arms and for being strong and great mentors in life.

To my partner in crime as kids, my brother, for seeming not to be scared of anything when we were kids, encouraging me to be more like him, fearless.

To my sister for being supportive and encouraging of me being able to write and compile this book, and for being the sensible one in the family.

To Doctor Julia Frearson (https://www.mindbodysantosha.co.uk) who without her constructive criticism, helpful suggestions, proof reading and support this book would not have the quality of content.

To Josh Downham, Paul Southgate and Melissa Clements for helping with some of the video footage and photographs taken for this book.

To Marc Ward for using his creativity and helping design the illustrations for this book. Who without I would have ended up with abstract drawings of a 4 year old.

To Hannah Williams for her photography and production skills to produce some of the photographs and videos linked in with this book.

To Mike Chrimes (www.michaelasher.co.uk) for his stunning photography skills and helping out in my hour of need.

To Mark Clubb (http://www.carmarmedia.co.uk) for his expertise and designing the cover of this book.

To the owners and staff from The Warehouse Climbing Centre (Gloucester) who allowed me to use the centre for some of the photography and most of the video footage used for this book.

To Luca Celano, an outdoor photographer and Mountaineering & Climbing instructor, for supplying a selection of beautiful photographs from his collection (https://lucaa3fa.myportfolio.com).

To Dave Talbot for attempting to read the first draft, and telling me he got bored, as it was too much waffle, and not enough story. Also for supplying a few pictures.

To Kieran Duncan, a professional photographer, who I have worked with closely for the last few years on a few projects, for supplying some stunning photographs for this book (check out his Instagram account @kieranjduncan).

To all of my friends and climbing partners for their mickey taking, sarcasm, pushing my limits, teaching me the way of the English humour and giving me their amazing friendship. Their hours of holding the ropes whilst I have been on the sharp end; scared, tired and mostly falling.

To Sam Jersche from SJ Editing (https://www.sjediting.com) for all of his hard work copy editing the content.

To Vicky Barlow (www.victoriabarlow.co.uk) for designing the beautiful layout of this book, and making me feel like a kid in a sweet shop, overexcited, once again.

To all of the athletes featured in the book who have contributed a picture and personal comment:

- Sandeep Kumar Maity
- Babsi Zangerl
- Emma Twyford
- Meagan Martin
- Miky Mawem
- Bassa Mawem
- Nasim Eshqi
- Nina Caprez
- Sean McColl
- Cailean Harker
- James Pearson
- Caroline Ciavaldini

To all of the photographers who have contributed stunning pictures included in this book:

- Kamil Sustiak – http://www.kamilsustiak.com
- Todd Tang – Instagram @Toddtang
- Diego Lopez – http://www.diegolopez.es/en
- Remi Fabregue – http://www.kros.fr
- Damien Largeron – https://www.damienlargeronphotography.com
- Moritz Latzka
- Vladek Zumr – https://www.vladekzumr.com
- Raph Fourau
- Pietro Porro
- Paul Wood
- Marc Daviet
- Marc Langley
- Sharad Chandra Khiyali
- David Penalva – http://www.davidpenalva.com
- Petr Slováček
- Cade Prior
- Christoph Deinet
- Bry Manning – Instagram @bry.manning
- Will Smith
- Damir Spanic
- Omid Armin
- Brett Jordan
- Victor Xok
- Ron Lach
- Maira Kouvara
- Elahe Motamedi
- José Mario
- Eddie Fowke – The Circuit Climbing
- Jeff Ochoa
- Fionn Claydon
- Angie Payne – https://www.angiepayne.com

To anyone else who has contributed pictures: Lary Arce, Melissa McDonald.

To anyone else who has supported me, inspired me and also allowed me to make my passion my job. Not sure you can call it a job...

References

CHAPTER 1

Ropeik, D. (2004), *The consequences of fear.* Available at: https://www.ncbi.nlm.nih.gov/pmc/articles/PMC1299209/

The brain from top to bottom, *The Amygdala and its allies.* Available at: https://thebrain.mcgill.ca/flash/i/i_04/i_04_cr/i_04_cr_peu/i_04_cr_peu.html

Dr Mandal, A., *What is the thalamus?* Available at: https://www.news-medical.net/health/What-is-the-Thalamus.aspx

Robb, A, *Somatosensory cortex: definition, location & function.* Available at: https://study.com/academy/lesson/somatosensory-cortex-definition-location-function.html

Anand, K.S. and Dhikav, V. (2012), *Hippocampus in health and disease: an overview.* Available at: https://www.ncbi.nlm.nih.gov/pmc/articles/PMC3548359/

Cherry, K. (2020), *Hippocampus role in the limbic system.* Available at: https://www.verywellmind.com/what-is-the-hippocampus-2795231

Williams, J. and Cena, C. (2020), *The Amygdala: Definition, role & function.* Available at: https://study.com/academy/lesson/the-amygdala-definition-role-function.html

Johnson, J. (2018), *What does the hypothalamus do?* Available at: https://www.medicalnewstoday.com/articles/312628.php

Newman, T. (2018), *Dissecting terror.* Available at: https://www.medicalnewstoday.com/articles/323492.php#1

Klucken, T. et al (2009), *Contingency Learning in Human Fear Conditioning Involves the Ventral Striatum.* Available at: https://pubmed.ncbi.nlm.nih.gov/19384886/

Elzinga, B. et al (2003), *Higher Cortisol Levels Following Exposure to Traumatic Reminders in Abuse-Related PTSD.* Available at: https://www.nature.com/articles/1300226

Delagran, L., *Impact of Fear and Anxiety.* Available at: https://www.takingcharge.csh.umn.edu/impact-fear-and-anxiety

Seltzer, L. (2015), *Trauma and the Freeze Response: Good, Bad, or Both?* Available at: https://www.psychologytoday.com/us/blog/évolution-the-self/201507/trauma-and-the-freeze-response-good-bad-or-both

Roelofs, K. (2017), *Freeze for action: neurobiological mechanisms in animal and human freezing.* Available at: https://www.ncbi.nlm.nih.gov/pmc/articles/PMC5332864/

Schmidt, N. et al (2007), *Exploring Human Freeze Responses to a Threat Stressor.* Available at: https://www.ncbi.nlm.nih.gov/pmc/articles/PMC2489204/

Westmeria (2019), *Understanding the freeze stress response.* Available at: https://westmeriacounselling.co.uk/understanding-the-freeze-stress-response/

Low, P. (2020), *Overview of the Autonomic Nervous System.* Available at: https://www.msdmanuals.com/en-gb/home/brain,-spinal-cord,-and-nerve-disorders/autonomic-nervous-system-disorders/overview-of-the-autonomic-nervous-system

Waxenbaum, J., Reddy, V. and Varacallo, M. (2020), *Anatomy, Autonomic Nervous System.* Available at: https://www.ncbi.nlm.nih.gov/books/NBK539845/

Oh, D.H. (2012), *Traumatic Experiences Disrupt Amygdala – Prefrontal Connectivity.* Available at: https://www.intechopen.com/books/the-amygdala-a-discrete-multitasking-manager/traumatic-experiences-disrupt-amygdala-prefrontal-connectivity

CHAPTER 2

McGrath, D. and Elison, J. (2014), *Vertical Mind – psychological approaches for Optimal Rock Climbing.* Sharp End Publishing

Dualdiagnosis.org, *How Trauma Affects the Human Body.* Available at: https://dualdiagnosis.org/mental-health-and-addiction/post-traumatic-stress-disorder-and-addiction/how-trauma-affects-the-human-body/

Chentsova-Dutton, Y. and Maercker, A. (2019), *Cultural Scripts of Traumatic Stress: Outline, Illustrations, and Research Opportunities.* Available at: https://www.ncbi.nlm.nih.gov/pmc/articles/PMC6872530/

Gardner, B. and Rebar, A. (2019), *Habit Formation and Behaviour Change.* Available at: https://oxfordre.com/psychology/view/10.1093/acrefore/9780190236557.001.0001/acrefore-9780190236557-e-129

Wood, W. and Neal, D. (2007), *A New Look at Habits and the Habit-Goal Interface.* Available at: https://www.researchgate.net/publication/5936907_A_New_Look_at_Habits_and_the_Habit-Goal_Interface

Schwartz, J. and Begley, S. (2004), *The Mind and the Brain: Neuroplasticity and the Power of Mental Force.* HarpPeren

Tull, M. (2020), *Recognizing Hyperarousal Symptoms in PTSD.* Available at: https://www.verywellmind.com/hyperarousal-2797362

Gardner, B., Lally, P. and Wardle, J. (2012), *Making health habitual: the psychology of 'habit-formation' and general practice.* Available at: https://www.ncbi.nlm.nih.gov/pmc/articles/PMC3505409/

Gladwell, M. (2008), Outliers. Little, Brown and company

CHAPTER 3

Rae-Dupree, J. (2008), *Can You Become a Creature of New Habits?* Available at: https://www.nytimes.com/2008/05/04/business/04unbox.html

Kerr, J. (1987), *Cognitive intervention with elite performers: Reversal theory.* British J Sports Med. Vol. 21, No.2

Salmansohn, K. (2001), *How to be happy dammit: a cynic's guide to spiritual happiness.* Celestial Arts

Gloud, D. and Krane, V. (1992), *The arousal–athletic performance relationship: Current status and future directions.* Human Kinetics Publishers.

Schoen, C.B. and Holtzer, R. (2016), *Differential Relationships of Somatic and Cognitive Anxiety with Measures of Processing Speed in Older Adults*. Available at: https://www.ncbi.nlm.nih.gov/pmc/articles/PMC5357197/

L. Abenza, F. Alarcon, M.I. Pinar, N. Urena (2009), *Relationship between the anxiety and performance on a basketball team during competition*. Revista de Psicología del Deporte, 18 (3) (2009), pp. 409-413

Fazey, J., and Hardy, L. (1988). *The inverted-U hypothesis: catastrophe for sport psychology*. British Association of Sports Sciences Monograph No. 1. Leeds: The National Coaching Foundation.

S. Gill, G.S. Kolt, J. Keating (2004), *Examining the multi-process theory: an investigation of the effects of two relaxation techniques on state anxiety.* Journal of Bodywork and Movement Therapies., 8 (4) (2004), pp. 288-296

Hardy, L., & Fazey, J. (1987). *The inverted U hypothesis: A Catastrophe for Sport Psychology*. The Annual Conference of The north American Society for the Psychology for sport and Physical Activity.

L. Hardy, G. Parfitt (1991), *A Catastrophe Model of Anxiety and Performance*. British Journal of Psychology., 82 (1991), pp. 163-178

Tenenbaum, G. and Eklund, R.C. (2020), *Handbook of sport psychology*. Fourth edition

Hanin, Y. L. (1997). *Emotions and athletic performance: Individual zones of optimal functioning model*. European Yearbook of Sport Psychology, 1, 29-72.

Hanin, Y. L. (2000). *Emotions in sport*. Champaign, IL: Human Kinetics.

CHAPTER 4

Scaccia, A. (2020), *Serotonin: What You Need to Know.* Available at: https://www.healthline.com/health/mental-health/serotonin#mental-health

Dietrich, A. (2003), *Functional neuroanatomy of altered states of consciousness: the transient hypofrontality hypothesis.* Available at: https://pubmed.ncbi.nlm.nih.gov/12763007/

Hall, E. et al (2010), *Cognitive Function During Acute Exercise: A Test of the Transient Hypofrontality Theory.* Available at: https://www.researchgate.net/profile/Eric_Hall3/publication/44851816_Cognitive_Function_During_Acute_Exercise_A_Test_of_the_Transient_Hypofrontality_Theory/links/0fcfd509a42250dd47000000/Cognitive-Function-During-Acute-Exercise-A-Test-of-the-Transient-Hypofrontality-Theory.pdf

Hays, K. (2017), *The Transient Hypofrontality Edge.* Available at: https://www.psychologytoday.com/gb/blog/the-edge-peak-performance-psychology/201703/the-transient-hypofrontality-edge

Ülrich, M. et al (2015), *Neural signatures of experimentally induced flow experiences identified in a typical fMRI block design with BOLD imaging.* Available at: https://www.researchgate.net/publication/283306869_Neural_signatures_of_experimentally_induced_flow_experiences_identified_in_a_typical_fMRI_block_design_with_BOLD_imaging

Kotler, S. (2014), *The Rise of Superman: Decoding the Science of Ultimate Human Performance.* Querqus.

Csíkszentmihályi, M. (2008), *Flow – the psychology of optimal experience.* Harper Perennial Modern Classics.

Bos, M., Dijksterhuis, A., and van Baaren, R. (2012), *Food for Thought? Trust Your Unconscious When Energy Is Low.* Available at: https://www.researchgate.net/publication/232550768_Food_for_Thought_Trust_Your_Unconscious_When_Energy_Is_Low

Dijksterhuis, A. et al (2009), *Predicting Soccer Matches After Unconscious and Conscious Thought as a Function of Expertise.* Available at: https://journals.sagepub.com/doi/abs/10.1111/j.1467-9280.2009.02451.x

Syed, M. (2017), *The Greatest: what sport teaches us about achieving success.* John Murray.

CHAPTER 5

West, H. (2017), *What Causes Fear of Failure and How to Conquer It with Self-Acceptance.* Available at: http://www.harperwest.co/what-causes-fear-of-failure-how-conquer-with-self-acceptance/

Winch, G. (2013), *10 Signs That You Might Have Fear of Failure.* Available at: https://www.psychologytoday.com/intl/blog/the-squeaky-wheel/201306/10-signs-you-might-have-fear-failure

Benninger, M. (2019), *The Psychology Behind Your Fear of Failure.* Available at: https://www.blinkist.com/magazine/posts/psychology-behind-fear-failure

Syed, M. (2015), *Black Box Thinking: The Surprising Truth About Success.* John Murray.

Syed, M. (2011), *Bounce: The Myth of Talent and the Power of Practice.* Fourth Estate GB.

Allerhand, R. (2019), *How to overcome fear of failure.* Available at: https://www.netdoctor.co.uk/healthy-living/mental-health/a26821636/fear-of-failure/

Mindtools.com, *Overcoming Fear of Failure Facing Your Fear of Moving Forward.* Available at: https://www.mindtools.com/pages/article/fear-of-failure.htm

McCarter, B. (2019), *How the Growth Mindset is Based on the Power of Failure.* Available at: https://medium.com/age-of-awareness/how-the-growth-mindset-is-based-on-the-power-of-failure-b44cb9269e2b

Mindsetworks.com, *Dr. Dweck's research into growth mindset changed education forever.* Available at: https://www.mindsetworks.com/science/

Dweck, C. (2015), *Carol Dweck Revisits the 'Growth Mindset'*. Available at: https://portal.cornerstonesd.ca/group/yyd5jtk/Documents/Carol%20 Dweck%20Growth%20Mindsets.pdf

Dweck, C. (2006). *Mindset: how you can fulfil your potential*. London: Constable & Robinson Ltd.

Davis, S. (2019), *The Neuroscience of Shame*. Available at: https://cptsdfoundation.org/2019/04/11/the-neuroscience-of-shame/

Berry, N. (2020), *Alex Megos on Bibliographie 9c*. Available at: https://www.ukclimbing.com/news/2020/09/alex_megos_on_bibliographie_9c-72476

CHAPTER 6

Kinderman, P. et al (2013), *Psychological Processes Mediate the Impact of Familial Risk, Social Circumstances and Life Events on Mental Health*. Available at: https://journals.plos.org/plosone/article?id=10.1371/journal.pone.0076564

Horn, T. (2008), *Advances in Sport psychology*. Champaign, IL: Human Kinetics.

Weinberg, R.S. and Gould, D. (2011), *Foundations of sport and exercise psychology*. Champaign, IL: Human Kinetics

Tod, D. et al (2011), *Effects of Self-Talk: A Systematic Review*. Available at: https://www.researchgate.net/publication/51704153_Effects_of_Self-Talk_A_Systematic_Review

Beck, A. (1963), *Thinking and depression: I. Idiosyncratic content and cognitive distortions*. Archives of General Psychiatry.

Beck, A. et al (1979), *Cognitive Therapy of Depression*. New York: Guilford press

Whalley, M. (2019), *Cognitive distortions: an introduction to how CBT describes unhelpful ways of thinking*. Available at: https://www.psychologytools.com/articles/unhelpful-thinking-styles-cognitive-distortions-in-cbt/

Tod, D. et al (2009), *Effects of Instructional and Motivational Self-Talk on the Vertical Jump*. Available at: https://journals.lww.com/nsca-jscr/fulltext/2009/01000/effects_of_instructional_and_motivational.30.aspx

Gallwey, W.T. (2015), *The inner Game of Tennis: The ultimate guide to the mental side of peak performance*. Pan Books

CHAPTER 7

Korthuis, R. and San, R. (2011), *Skeletal Muscle Circulation – Chapter 4Exercise Hyperemia and Regulation of Tissue Oxygenation During Muscular Activity.* Available at: https://www.ncbi.nlm.nih.gov/books/NBK57139/

Osada, T. and Rådegran, G., *Difference in muscle blood flow fluctuations between dynamic and static thigh muscle contractions: How to evaluate exercise blood flow by Doppler ultrasound.* Available at: https://www.oatext.com/Difference-in-muscle-blood-flow-fluctuations-between-dynamic-and-static-thigh-muscle-contractions-How-to-evaluate-exercise-blood-flow-by-Doppler-ultrasound.php#gsc.tab=0

Rigby, B. (2015), *Learn This: The Over-Gripping Myth.* Available at: https://www.climbing.com/skills/learn-this-the-over-gripping-myth/

Robergs, A. et al (2004), *Biochemistry of exercise-induced metabolic acidosis.* Available at: https://pubmed.ncbi.nlm.nih.gov/15308499/

Klabunde, R. (2010), *Skeletal Muscle Blood Flow.* Available at: https://www.cvphysiology.com/Blood%20Flow/BF015

Van der Hörst, E. (2016), *Training for Climbing: The Definitive Guide to Improving Your Performance*. Falcon Guides.

CHAPTER 8

Russo, M. et al (2017), *The physiological effects of slow breathing in the healthy human.* Available at: https://www.ncbi.nlm.nih.gov/pmc/articles/PMC5709795/

Watkins, A. (2014), *Benefits of deep breathing.* Available at: https://urbanbalance.com/benefits-deep-breathing/

The University of Dublin (2018), *The Yogi masters were right – breathing exercises can sharpen your mind.* Available at: https://www.tcd.ie/news_events/articles/the-yogi-masters-were-right-breathing-exercises-can-sharpen-your-mind/

Cap, A. (2013), *The Nose Knows: A Case for Nasal Breathing During High Intensity Exercise.* Available at: https://adamcap.com/2013/11/29/the-nose-knows/

Sano, M. et al (2013), *Increased oxygen load in the prefrontal cortex from mouth breathing: a vector-based near-infrared spectroscopy study.* Available at: https://www.ncbi.nlm.nih.gov/pmc/articles/PMC4047298/

Chang, H. et al (2013), *Effects of blood flow to the prefrontal cortex on high-intensity exercise combined with high-decibel music.* Available at: https://www.ncbi.nlm.nih.gov/pmc/articles/PMC4241909/

Ulrich, M. et al (2015), *Neural signatures of experimentally induced flow experiences identified in a typical fMRI block design with BOLD imaging.* Available at: https://www.researchgate.net/publication/283306869_Neural_signatures_of_experimentally_induced_flow_experiences_identified_in_a_typical_fMRI_block_design_with_BOLD_imaging

Dickerson, H. (2017), *Nitric Oxide and mouth breathing.* Available at: https://www.lviglobal.com/wp-content/uploads/2017/06/NitricOxideMouthBreathing.pdf

Nestor, J. (2020), *Breath: The new science of a lost art.* Penguin publishing.

Marksberry, K. (2012), *Take a Deep Breath.* Available at: https://www.stress.org/take-a-deep-breath

Princing, M. (2018), *This Is Why Deep Breathing Makes You Feel so Chill.* Available at: https://rightasrain.uwmedicine.org/mind/stress/why-deep-breathing-makes-you-feel-so-chill

Lundberg, J. (2002), *Nasal and oral contribution to inhaled and exhaled nitric oxide: a study in tracheotomised patients.* European respiration journal

Russo, M. et al (2017), *The physiological effects of slow breathing in the healthy human.* Available at: https://www.ncbi.nlm.nih.gov/pmc/articles/PMC5709795/

Recinto, C. et al (2017), *Effects of Nasal or Oral Breathing on Anaerobic Power Output and Metabolic Responses.* Available at: https://www.ncbi.nlm.nih.gov/pmc/articles/PMC5466403/

Dallam, G. and Kies, B. (2020), *The Effect of Nasal Breathing Versus Oral and Oronasal Breathing During Exercise: A Review.* Available at: https://www.researchgate.net/publication/338558548_The_Effect_of_Nasal_Breathing_Versus_Oral_and_Oronasal_Breathing_During_Exercise_A_Review

Zaccaro, A. et al (2018), *How Breath-Control Can Change Your Life: A Systematic Review on Psycho-Physiological Correlates of Slow Breathing.* Available at: https://www.ncbi.nlm.nih.gov/pmc/articles/PMC6137615/

Shaffer, J. (2016), *Neuroplasticity and Clinical Practice: Building Brain Power for Health.* Available at: https://www.ncbi.nlm.nih.gov/pmc/articles/PMC4960264/

CHAPTER 10

Ostwald, P.F. (1959), *When people whistle.* Available at: https://doi.org/10.1177/002383095900200303

Ericsson, K.A. and Harwell, K.W. (2019), *Deliberate Practice and Proposed Limits on the Effects of Practice on the Acquisition of Expert Performance: Why the Original Definition Matters and Recommendations for Future Research.* Frontiers in Psychology.

CHAPTER 11

Ilgner, A. (2006), *The Rock Warrior's Way: Mental Training for Climbers.* Desiderata Inst

CHAPTER 13

Cotterill, S. et al (2008), *Developing Effective Pre-performance Routines in Golf: Why Don't We Ask the Golfer?* Available at: https://www.tandfonline.com/doi/abs/10.1080/10413200903403216

Cox, R. (1986), *Psychological preparation for competition – mental Rehearsal.* Edinburgh: The Scottish Sports Council.

Cumming, J., & Williams, S. E. (2012), *The role of imagery in performance. Handbook of sport and performance psychology.* New York: Oxford University Press.

Ryan, F. (1981), *Sports and psychology.* Englewood Cliffs, Prentice Hall Inc.

Minas, S. (1978), *Mental practice of a complex perceptual motor skill.* Journal of human movement studies.

Yao, Q., Xu, F. and Lin, J. (2020), *A Qualitative Study on Pre-performance Routines of Diving: Evidence From Elite Chinese Diving Athletes.* Available at: https://www.frontiersin.org/articles/10.3389/fpsyg.2020.00193/full

Bleak, J. and Frederick, C. (1998), *Superstitious behavior in sport: Levels of effectiveness and determinants of use in three collegiate sports.* Available at: https://www.researchgate.net/publication/292810172_Superstitious_behavior_in_sport_Levels_of_effectiveness_and_determinants_of_use_in_three_collegiate_sports

Morton, P. (2003), *The Hypnotic Belay in Alpine Mountaineering: The Use of Self-Hypnosis for the Resolution of Sports Injuries and for Performance Enhancement.* Available at: https://www.asch.net/portals/0/journallibrary/articles/ajch-46/morton.pdf

McNeal, S., and Frederick, C. (1993), *Inner strength and other techniques for ego- strengthening.* American Journal of Clinical Hypnosis.

Otani, A. (2003), *Eastern Meditative Techniques and Hypnosis: A New Synthesis.* Available at: https://www.asch.net/portals/0/journallibrary/articles/ajch-46/otani.pdf?origin%3Dpublication_detail

Kettle J. (2018), *Rock Climbing Technique: The practical guide to movement mastery.* John Kettle

Scott, M.W., Wright, D.J., Smith, D. and Holmes, P.S. (2022), *Twenty years of PETTLEP imagery: An update and new direction for simulation-based training.* Asian Journal of Sport and Exercise Psychology, Vol. 2, Issue 2, 70-79

Ali, S.A., Begum, T. and Reza, F. (2018), *Hormonal influences on cognitive function.* Available at: https://www.ncbi.nlm.nih.gov/pmc/articles/PMC6422548/

Elliott, D., Polman, R. and Taylor, J. (2012), *The effects of relaxing music for anxiety control on competitive sport anxiety.* Available at: https://pubmed.ncbi.nlm.nih.gov/24444221/

Kuan, G., Morris, T. and Terry, P. (2017), *Effects of music on arousal during imagery in elite shooters: A pilot study.* Available at: https://www.ncbi.nlm.nih.gov/pmc/articles/PMC5393549/

Hollins, P. (2022), *The brain mechanic: Achieve Peak mental performance, neurogroth, and cognitive fitness.*

Perry, J. (2015), *Sport Psychology: a complete introduction.* Hodder & Stoughton

Peden, A. (2007), *Managing Performance anxiety in Tennis.* Trafford Publishing

Hanin, Y. (2010), *Coping with anxiety in sport.* Available at: https://www.researchgate.net/publication/235947366_Coping_with_anxiety_in_sport

Dishman, R.K., Washburn, R.A. and Heath, G.W. (2004), *Physical Activity Epidemiology.* Champaign: Human Kinetics, 338

Bahrke, M.S. and Morgan, W.P. (1978), *Anxiety Reduction Following Exercise and Meditation.* Cognitive Therapy and Research 2, no. 4

Zuckerman, M. (1978), *The Search for High Sensation.* Psychology Today 11, no. 9

Brown, R.P. and Gerbarg, P.L. (2005), *Sudarshan Kriya Yogic Breathing in the Treatment of Stress, Anxiety, and Depression: Part II - Clinical Applications and Guidelines.* Journal of Alternative and Complementary Medicine 11, no. 4

Levitt, J.H. (2011), *Conquering Anxiety, Depression, and Fatigue Without Drugs – the Role of Hypoglycemia*. Available at: http://www.alternativementalhealth.com/articles/hypoglycemia.htm

Holmes, P. S., and Collins, D. J. (2001), *The PETTLEP approach to motor imagery: A functional equivalence model for sport psychologists*. Journal of Applied Sport Psychology

Smith, D., Holmes, P., Whitemore, L., Collins, D., and Devonport, T. (2001), *The effect of theoretically-based imagery scripts on field hockey performance*. Journal of Sport Behaviour

Smith, D., Wright, C. J., Allsopp, A. and Westhead, H. (2007), *It's all in the mind: PETTLEP-based imagery and sports performance*. Journal of Applied Sport Psychology

Smith, D., Wright, C.J. and Cantwell, C. (2008), *Beating the bunker: The effect of PETTLEP imagery on golf bunker shot performance*. Research Quarterly for Exercise and Sport

Wilson, C., Smith, D., Holmes, P., and Burden, A. (2010), *Participant-generated imagery scripts produce greater EMG activity and imagery ability*. European Journal of Sport Sciences

Thoma, M.V., La Marca, R., Brönnimann, R., Finkel, L., Ehlert, U. and Nater, U.M. (2013), *The Effect of Music on the Human Stress Response*. Available at: https://www.ncbi.nlm.nih.gov/pmc/articles/PMC3734071/

Bernardi, L., Porta, C. and Sleight, P. (2006), *Cardiovascular, cerebrovascular, and respiratory changes induced by different types of music in musicians and non-musicians: the importance of silence*. Available at: https://www.ncbi.nlm.nih.gov/pmc/articles/PMC1860846/

Salo, A. (2019), *The Power of Dance: How Dance Effects Mental and Emotional Health and Self-Confidence in Young Adults*. University of Northern Colorado

Gothe, N.P., Khan, I., Hayes, J., Erlenbach, E. and Damoiseaux, J.S. (2019), *Yoga Effects on Brain Health: A Systematic Review of the Current Literature*. Available at: https://www.ncbi.nlm.nih.gov/pmc/articles/PMC6971819/

Kay, A.D., Husbands-Beasley, J. and Blazevich, A.J. (2015), *Effects of Contract-Relax, Static Stretching, and Isometric Contractions on Muscle-Tendon Mechanics*. Available at: https://pubmed.ncbi.nlm.nih.gov/25668401/

Van Gelder, L.H. and Bartz, S.D. (2011), *The Effect of Acute Stretching on Agility Performance*. Available at: https://journals.lww.com/nsca-jscr/fulltext/2011/11000/the_effect_of_acute_stretching_on_agility.11.aspx

Hardy, J. (2006), *Speaking clearly: A critical review of the self-talk literature*. Psychology of Sport and Exercise

Hatzigeorgiadis, A., Zourbanos, N., Galanis, E. and Theodorakis, Y. (2011), *Self-talk and sports performance: A meta-analysis*. Perspectives on Psychological Science

Hatzigeorgiadis, A., Zourbanos, N., Galanis, E. and Theodorakis, Y. (2014). *Self-talk and competitive sport performance*. Journal of Applied Sport Psychology

Walter, N., Nikoleizig, L. and Alfermann, D. (2019), *Effects of Self-Talk Training on Competitive Anxiety, Self-Efficacy, Volitional Skills, and Performance: An Intervention Study with Junior Sub-Elite Athletes*. Available at: https://www.ncbi.nlm.nih.gov/pmc/articles/PMC6628429/

Index

D

E

F

G

H

I

K

L

M

N

O

P

R

S

T

U

V

W

Y

Z